CRITICAL APPROPRIATIONS

SOUTHERN LITERARY STUDIES
Scott Romine, Series Editor

SIMONE C. DRAKE

CRITICAL APPROPRIATIONS

African American Women and the Construction
of Transnational Identity

Louisiana State University Press
Baton Rouge

Published by Louisiana State University Press
Copyright © 2014 by Louisiana State University Press
All rights reserved
Manufactured in the United States of America
First printing

Designer: Michelle A. Neustrom
Typeface: Whitman
Printer and binder: Maple Press

Portions of chapter two first appeared as "Gendering Diasporic Migration in
Erna Brodber's *Louisiana.*" *MaComère: The Journal of the Association of Caribbean
Women Writers and Scholars* 8 (2006): 112–135.

Library of Congress Cataloging-in-Publication Data

Drake, Simone C., 1975–
   Critical appropriations : African American women and the construction of
transnational identity / Simone C. Drake.
      pages cm. — (Southern Literary Studies)
   Includes bibliographical references and index.
   ISBN 978-0-8071-5387-1 (cloth : alk. paper) — ISBN 978-0-8071-5388-8
(pdf) — ISBN 978-0-8071-5389-5 (epub) — ISBN 978-0-8071-5390-1 (mobi)
   1. American literature—African American authors—History and criticism.
2. American literature—Women authors—History and criticism. 3. Women,
Black—Race identity. 4. Women, Black, in literature. 5. African diaspora in
literature. I. Title.
   PS153.N5D73 2014
   810.9'928708996073—dc23

                                                                    2013024531

The paper in this book meets the guidelines for permanence and
durability of the Committee on Production Guidelines for Book
Longevity of the Council on Library Resources. ∞

For Seth, Isaac, and Solon—my beautiful boys.

CONTENTS

ACKNOWLEDGMENTS

I have been blessed to have had the immense support of family, friends, mentors, and colleagues on this journey. Words can only capture a fraction of my gratitude. This book began as a dissertation but has been heavily revised. I extend thanks to Kandice Chuh, Gene Jarrett, Shirley Wilson Logan, and A. Lynn Bolles, my dissertation committee members at the University of Maryland. Special thanks go to David Wyatt for directing my dissertation and helping me to trust my own ideas and "keep it simple." The recovery work and prolific contributions Mary Helen Washington has made to black women's studies and to pushing me to produce at my fullest potential is greatly appreciated.

I have learned that there are those whose support is explicit, and then, there are those who work behind the scenes, supporting you and advocating for you when you might not even know you need it. Ansley Abraham, director of the SREB—State Doctoral Scholars Program—has done both. SREB provided much-needed fellowship support for four years of my graduate study, but the mentoring support Dr. Abraham and his team provided rival anything money can provide. Johnetta Davis listened and helped when I needed it. Carol Henderson affirmed my work and made me feel good about myself as a scholar, mother, wife, and black woman. In spite of an unbelievably busy schedule, Valerie Lee has always been there when I needed guidance, both as a student and now as a colleague. Maurice Stevens has always seen the glass half full. Joseph McLaughlin and Amritjit Singh provided guidance during my postdoctoral fellowship at Ohio University. John Jackson and Toni King not only selected me as a dissertation fellow at Denison University, but they also became dear friends whose guidance on work and life emphasized the importance of having a life outside of work. Special thanks go to Anthonia Kalu, the department chair at OSU when I was hired, and to Ike Newsum, my current chair. Both have been supportive and thoughtful regarding my needs as a junior faculty member.

I have had the privilege of many friends and colleagues offering me feedback on this book. Dwan Henderson Simmons and Deonne Minto are brilliant readers and thinkers whose critical feedback always makes my work stronger. Terry Rowden has offered feedback that was strategic and invaluable for moving this project from dissertation to book. Linda Krumholz read and reread a chapter, and her feedback not only made me a better writer but also taught me some things about myself as a writer. Marlene Tromp, Anita Waters, Ayesha Hardison, Kalenda Eaton, and Jackie Royster all read chapters too. At the end of this journey, I was fortunate to have the benefit of presenting the project at a workshop hosted by the Diversity Enhancement Program at OSU. Ruby Tapia and Rebecca Wanzo provided detailed feedback that took me from being almost "there" to really being "there," as I completed my revisions. Chadwick Allen, Andrea Williams, Theresa Delgadillo, Pranav Jani, and Lynn Itagaki raised important questions during the workshop that helped to shape the final production. And seasoned publishing knowledge informed the feedback provided by Valerie Lee and Adélékè Adéèkó.

Having to learn how to teach the concepts I was writing about was a worthwhile challenge, and there are certain students who made it pleasurable. Terrance Wooten, Faouzie Alchahal, and Jasmine McGhee are all brilliant students who provided me with the opportunity to mentor them and think critically about what it means to be a scholar and teacher. And, they loved my babies.

Andrew Drake, my confidant, best friend, and balancing agent, has been by my side as I traversed the vicissitudes of graduate school and an academic career. He has read my work, listened to presentations, and offered unexpected, yet thoughtful critiques of my scholarship, daring to disagree at times when I only wanted praise. Our precious little ones— Seth, Isaac, and Solon—who all spent time on my lap as I produced this book have sustained me emotionally through the joys (and hard work) of motherhood. My sister, Natalie Poindexter, has loved my babies and been on call uncountable times to help me succeed at my professional endeavors. My brother, Jason Poindexter, has helped when needed. My parents, Edward and Dianna Poindexter, encouraged me to love learning and made countless sacrifices to enable me to do what I do, but most importantly, they read to me every night as a child. My in-laws, Barbara Drake Showalter and Dr. John Showalter, have often wondered when I would be "done" and offered support through the process.·

Some friends are family. Dr. Viola Newton came into my life when I needed her more than I realized. She has been a friend, mentor, confidant, mother, and fierce advocate. She has adopted me and my family as her own, providing wonderful meals, wise counsel, and when needed, the hard truths that make you a better person. Her persistent belief in my ideas, my teaching, my parenting skills, and my capabilities has sustained me. It can only be grace that sent Jesse J. Scott into my life. We have navigated graduate school and academe together, and we are both still standing. His intellectual generosity has been bottomless; his engagement of my ideas invaluable. More meaningful, he has rocked my babies, shared my pleasure in finding good food, made me laugh (a lot), and reminded me not to forget about me. I am grateful to have found such a dear friend and lucky to have found one with such a beautiful mind and compassionate soul.

Finally, I would like to thank John Easterly, former executive editor at Louisiana State University Press, for his encouragement and belief in my project. Upon his retirement, his successor, Margaret Lovecraft, has been equally supportive and helpful through this process. I am indebted to my reviewers and the Southern Literary Studies series editors, Fred Hobson and Scott Romine, for their feedback and guidance.

CRITICAL APPROPRIATIONS

A s both a concept and a practice, defining *transnationalism* has been and continues to be a vexed project for scholars. Academic disciplines, geographic focus, and political goals function as critical factors in how scholars have defined and specified who and what are transnational. In spite of the different agendas and ideologies that guide the various approaches to exploring transnationalism, explorations have focused heavily and almost exclusively on immigration and migration. Privileging of travel and physical movement across geographical boundaries has been at the heart of transnational studies. This study is decidedly not about immigration, migration, or physical travel or movement; yet, it is wholly invested in the transnational. *Critical Appropriations: African American Women and the Construction of Transnational Identity* considers the ways in which a variety of black women artists create cultural productions that negotiate how transnationalism is understood as a concept and as a practice. I argue that the black women artists I study are intervening in the dominant discourse of transnational studies that fails to register a relationship between transnationalism and African Americans whose families have resided in the United States for generations.[1] Erna Brodber, Toni Morrison, Beyoncé Knowles, Danzy Senna, Gayl Jones, and Kasi Lemmons all offer cultural productions that present characters or performances that claim transnational identities for African American women who do not travel, women who stay put in the United States.

The idea of a transnational identity that is not framed by travel, or *immobile transnationalism*, is not as paradoxical as it might seem. The notion of "rooted cosmopolitanism" espoused by Kwame Anthony Appiah in *The Ethics of Identity* proposes that one can simultaneously have roots that are embedded in a particular local culture and history while also being a citizen of the world. Through this view, local histories are not shaped in a bubble; people and their cultural practices influence the development of local views. In fact, I would argue that all transnationalisms work in this manner, even when mobility is privileged in the discourse that attends to them.

Extending the notion that local histories and views are not developed in isolation, Arjun Appadurai frames *Modernity at Large: Cultural Dimensions of Globalization* with the premise that intersocietal relations have ruptured over the last few decades. This theory demonstrates how modern subjectivity is informed by "two major, and interconnected, diacritics and [Appadurai] explores their joint effect on the *work of the imagination*" (3). Electronic media, Appadurai argues, has changed the larger field of mass media and other traditional media, resulting in the construction of imagined selves and imagined worlds. The ability to imagine in such a manner transforms "everyday discourse" and produces "characters for new social projects, and not just a counterpoint to the certainties of daily life" (3, 6). The way that Appadurai articulates the imagination as a space that facilitates agency—the ability to act—and not simply a fantasy realm wherein one might escape from reality is an understanding that is critical to how the black women artists I study approach claiming a space in transnational discourse.

Both Appiah and Appadurai theorize the transnational flow of culture in ways that explicate how one might develop a transnational epistemological framework through which one lives and understands the world without traveling across national boundaries. An area of study that has made pointed efforts to engage the paradox of immobility and transnationalism is American studies.[2] At the close of the twentieth century, American studies began expanding its intellectual focus beyond the incorporation of past and present disparate ethnic cultures of the United States in order to consider how the transnational fit into the field. The interrogation of the discipline resulted in nearly ten years of American Studies Association (ASA) presidential addresses that consider what Shelley Fisher Fishkin termed "the transnational turn in American Studies" in her 2004 address. Fishkin predicts that, once the transnational moves to the center of American studies, the work of someone like Arthur Alfonso Schomburg and the intellectual, multilingual place in which he dwelled will be the rule—"a place where the diasporic imaginations are valued for the dazzlingly hybrid syntheses they produce" (26).[3] While Fishkin initially does what is often the case in these discussions when her references consistently note texts, scholars, and cultural phenomena that are circumscribed by physical travel, migration, and national border crossing, she briefly moves out of that framework and makes a poignant point about ideas traveling both into the United States and out of the country to other places (28). It is commonly acknowledged that the transnational flow of culture is transmitted through the actual physical bodies that move across borders, but an inevitable fact of human existence, though many often attribute this phenomenon to modernity, is that the transnational flow of culture is also transmitted through the movement of ideas, independent of actual bodies. The critical advances in technology in the late twentieth and early twenty-first centuries create an opportunity for the vast transmission of ideas between cultures without physical movement.

The black women artists I highlight in this study produce texts that register the influence modernity and new technologies have had on the transnational flow of culture. What is important about these particular texts is that they function as analytics; they challenge scholars to think critically about how the transnational is framed. I contend that the act of claiming and creating a transnational identity without traveling, troubles numerous fields of study in which African American women have been and continue to be positioned at the margins. The transnational thus becomes a libratory tool in these women's art; it allows them a creative space not only to create alternative epistemologies, but also to redefine notions of community and family in ways that enable them to embrace a more complex, transnational blackness at the dawning of the twenty-first century.

Critical Appropriations is an interdisciplinary project that analyzes the ways particular black women's cultural productions demonstrate an investment in constructing a transnational identity for African American women who do not travel, women who "stay put" within the United States. De-centering the U.S. nation and analyzing African American women's cultural productions through a transnational lens create a local home space for both the artists and for the African American subjects they create. A close examination of Toni Morrison's novel *Paradise*, Danzy

Senna's novel *Caucasia,* Gayl Jones's novel *Corregidora,* Erna Brodber's novel *Louisiana,* Kasi Lemmons's film *Eve's Bayou,* and Beyoncé Knowles's *B-Day* CD and music-video collaboration with Shakira, "Beautiful Liar," reveals how concepts of créolité, Candomblé, négritude, Latinidad, Brasilidade, and hybridity are appropriated in the work of these artists as a way of replacing the race-based oppositional paradigm of black cultural studies with a flexible, transnational framework, which allows for more nuanced considerations of community, mobility, and gender.

Community, mobility, and gender have played significant roles in limiting scholarly understandings of African American women as possessing any diasporic or transnational sensibilities. I propose the act of positioning the cultural productions of African American women at the center of contemporary transnational discourse, or, re-inventing transnational studies, illuminates an often overlooked contribution to the field that can produce a more nuanced understanding of transnationalism. What I propose is not a hierarchy for which one marginalized group should be centered; instead, similar to Mary Helen Washington's 1997 presidential address to the American Studies Association, my proposal contends that new and radical understandings of the field itself will emerge when African American women are centered in transnational studies.[4]

This centering is inherent in what I refer to as "critical appropriations." I use the adjective "critical" because I recognize these appropriations as being strategic and intentional. While the artists do not express their intent, the content of their narratives reflects a commitment to understanding that some African Americans embody a transnational blackness that reflects the "hybrid syntheses" Fishkin predicts will occur without physical travel. The African American women in the texts I examine are U.S. citizens, but a transnational sensibility defines their identities, as various diasporic theories travel and move across international borders both through the bodies that are moving across these borders and through the technologies that also perpetuate the transnational flow of culture. A transnational sensibility, then, informs the epistemological frameworks of the characters and performers, making it shortsighted to neglect such individuals in transnational studies. In other words, the inclusion in transnational studies of African American women who do not make home spaces outside the United States but possess transnational sensibilities is an asset to the field because such inclusion will produce more nuanced and complex understandings of what constitutes a transnational identity.

These critical appropriations are influenced by a diaspora consciousness that situates these acts as something more than merely artistic creativity, but rather as political acts that have historically marked African American women's cultural productions. The political acts are acts of truth telling as resistance that African American women have practiced in written forms since the nineteenth-century production of slave narratives.[5] These critical appropriations by African American women represent a continuum of writing and artistic production practices that tell the truth about African American women's relationship to both the nation and the world. The truth telling that takes place in the texts I examine offers African American women readers the opportunity to also construct a transnational identity through the practice of reading and viewing work by the authors. And, like the texts I examine, African American women readers can embody a transnational black identity without movement, which is a particularly important point when considering the popularity of black women's reading clubs over the past twenty years.[6]

IMMOBILE TRANSNATIONALISM

Like many fields of study, scholarship on black women's studies at the turn of the twenty-first century sought to assess the state of the field. An important issue that arises is the place of the field within other fields of cultural inquiry, particularly black and diaspora studies, women's studies, and transnational studies. Over thirty years have passed since Barbara Smith's pivotal essay, "Toward a Black Feminist Criticism," laid the groundwork for how the cultural work of black women is assessed and analyzed.[7] A critical paradigm shift in cultural studies has taken place since Smith and other scholars identified race-based tropes of family, kinship, and community as essential framing elements in black women's cultural productions.[8] Now, "race projects" are often castigated as regressive, as discourse on race and culture has turned from national-oriented identity politics to interrogations of the post-national and post-identity subject positions people of color in the United States occupy. *Critical Appropriations* contributes to the paradigm shift from national to post-national by

investigating the ways in which critical appropriations of diasporic theories of cultural identity in cultural productions produced by black women
creates transnational identities in African American women who embrace
a diaspora consciousness. Such a maneuver positions black women's
studies at the center of critical discourse in black and diaspora studies,
women's studies, and transnational studies, rather than marginalized at the
periphery—a location often forced upon black women.

The act of constructing a transnational identity without traveling is
one that the artists I examine inherited. Many African American women
may be understood as transnational *subjects* because they did in fact travel
across national boundaries—Zora Neale Hurston, Josephine Baker, and
Anna Julia Cooper traveled and lived outside of the United States and
ultimately became transnational subjects. Pauline Hopkins, the late-
nineteenth and early twentieth-century novelist, editor, and race woman
is perhaps the most compelling example of an intellectual and creative
precursor to the women I study because she constructed a transnational
identity from right here in the United States. Her serial novel *Of One
Blood* proposes that, in order for African Americans—an anachronistic
term for that time—to free their minds, they needed alternative ways of
understanding their blackness. *Of One Blood* provides an alternative epistemology, as a significant portion of the text is set in Ethiopia. Although
her protagonist, Reuell Briggs, a medical student who has no interest in
his African heritage, does indeed travel outside the United States, Hopkins herself does not; she instead imagines a way of knowing that she
hopes might free African Americans from racial degradation in the United
States. Similarly, yet differently, Angela Davis and Assata Shakur embody
a transnational identity through the ways in which their political ideologies have traveled outside of the country and influenced Afro-Cuban resistance movements, without their bodies necessarily traveling.[9]

It is significant that these formations of transnational identities are
situated in literature, performance, and politics, spaces that facilitate
change through the use of the imagination. The ability to change something is first dependent upon one's ability to imagine something different.
Literature, performance, and politics are ideal spaces for laying out blue-
prints for alternative realities and viewpoints. The women in this study,
like their precursor, Hopkins, are invested in re-imagining community

and family in ways that can offer African American women the possibility of, to appropriate Wendy Walters's term, "being at home in diaspora."[10]

In Toni Morrison's essay "Home," she discusses the troubling dialectical relationship between race and the construction of "a-world-in-which-race-does-*not*-matter," or "home," as she calls it. Morrison notes that, if she has to live in what she calls a "racial house," then it is necessary "to rebuild it so that it was not a windowless prison into which I was forced, a thick-walled, impenetrable container from which no cry could be heard, but rather an open house, grounded, yet generous in its supply of windows and doors" (3–4). The rebuilding of a racial house implies the need for safety—the need to locate or create a "social space that is psychically and physically safe" (10). The artists I examine are searching for just such a safe social space; yet, their search is compounded by gender. It is both their raced *and* gendered bodies that produce a discomfort in the nation as well as in their racial communities. The idea of critical appropriations of diasporic theories of cultural identity is thus not only about identifying alternative ways of knowing that produce more complex black identities without traveling. Critical appropriations and the knowledge gained through the act are also about the intersections of gender with race and the challenges that African American women face when working to construct an identity and locate a home place in a racialized, patriarchal nation.

This analysis of critical appropriations in the cultural productions of African American women troubles tropes of family genealogy and kinship that privilege a homogenous black community. Disrupting notions of homogeneity and essentialist notions of racialized communities negotiates an imaginative and radical space for African American women that offers the possibility of transforming a "race house," as Morrison calls it, into a home space that is, to borrow Morrison's words, "snug and wide open," not just for raced people, but for people who have been both raced *and* gendered. When Beyoncé appropriates Latinidad on her *B-Day* CD and in her "Beautiful Liar" video collaboration with Shakira, her appropriation situates herself and her art in a transnational context as opposed to a race-based national framework. The appropriation benefits her seemingly on a personal level as well as on a business level because non-immigrant black women who maintain their home in the United States are not understood as embodying transnational identities. Theories of négritude are appropriated in Erna Brodber's *Louisiana* in order to make the United States a home that replaces the idea of a local community or national allegiance and instead privileges a Pan-African community of activists, artists, and everyday people. Similar to *Louisiana*, Kasi Lemmons's *Eve's Bayou* attends to the specific implications of Louisiana, the U.S. state, as a hybrid cultural and racial geography. Unlike Brodber, though, in *Eve's Bayou*, emphasis is placed on the fissures produced by hybridity through the trope of incest—a trope that critically challenges theories of négritude and Pan-Africanism. *Caucasia* and *Corregidora* offer a critical re-evaluation of kinship, family, and community when Danzy Senna and Gayl Jones interrogate the principles of Brazilianness or Brasilidade and the pitfalls that arise when ideologies framing Brazil's racial-democracy propaganda travel, quite literally, to the United States.

Toni Morrison appropriates and syncretizes a number of diasporic cultural theories of identity—négritude, hybridity, Brazilianness, and créolité—in *Paradise*. Her syncretic appropriation of diasporic and European religious epistemologies suggests that black subjects are not only able to travel without leaving home, but they can also be "at home in diaspora." Appropriation, however, is a complicated and often political act. My analyses necessarily attend to the risks and benefits of critical appropriations, considering how the various appropriations assist the artists in constructing a more complex understanding of how race and geography interact globally, while also considering some of the pitfalls produced when one marginalized group appropriates cultural theories of other marginalized groups.

TROUBLING RACE, TROUBLING DIASPORA

A logical component of the post-national paradigm that now frames cultural discourse is the castigation of "race projects." The term "race project" is rather nebulous, but it is often used to describe texts, arguments, and theoretical frameworks that privilege discussions of race in a manner that is invested in understanding the *inclining* significance of race. In other words, the increasingly popular post-race rhetoric that in many ways found a comfortable and accepted space in cultural and media discourse after the election of President Barack Obama, the nation's first African American president, insists that racial equality has been reached and race no longer dictates the social, political, and economic experiences of racial minorities in the United States. Whether one accepts this rhetoric or not, it is difficult, if not impossible, to analyze the status of black womanhood during any cultural moment without attending to her raced and gendered subject position. This of course is true of discussions on black manhood, too. So, for example, why is there a persistence in what is becoming known as post-identity discourse to highlight all of the multifarious ways in which "black" is "black no more?"[11] This question is complicated, and there are many diverging approaches to answering it, but at the heart of the question is the issue of essentialism.

Madhu Dubey insists that heterogeneity is at the heart of post-national discourse when she asserts that new forms of political solidarity must be formed—solidarities that move beyond race and nation and include class, gender, and sexuality. "The question of how to develop a collective racial politics that gives due weight to intra-racial differences," Dubey argues, "forms the central challenge of the postmodern era in African-American culture and politics" ("Postmodernism as Postnationalism?" 5).[12] The point Dubey makes rings true for African American women artists in the postmodern era. In order to move from the periphery, African American women artists must formulate ways to represent and imagine the complexity of an African American subjectivity beyond the highly racialized, homogenous construction of blackness. Critical appropriations of theories of diasporic cultural identity carve out a space in black cultural discourse for heterogeneous "postmodern formulations of the problem of racial representation" (12). The heterogeneity of African Americans is highlighted when artists move away from the tropes of family genealogy and kinship that were central to the cultural productions of African American women during the 1970s, 1980s, and into the 1990s. Each text I examine depicts communities and individuals who look elsewhere or beyond national boundaries for constructs that negotiate their geopolitical positions without actually leaving home. As such, earlier ideas of community, kinship, and family are disrupted.

The concept of *diaspora* might initially seem a more appropriate term for theorizing the phenomenon. Diaspora, like the term *transnational*, is framed by the idea of movement. The reality is that both terms work in tandem with one another in the ways that African American women are excluded from the discourse surrounding these concepts. If not examined critically, the concept of *diaspora* can suggest endless continuities between people who have been dispersed from the same geographical location. While various definitions and theories of diaspora exist, my concept of an African diaspora begins with the Greek derivation of the term from *dispersal,* or to be scattered abroad.[13] By emphasizing dispersal, the theories of diaspora that I find most useful are those that understand the African diaspora as being composed of those who have been dispersed from Africa either by force through indentured servitude, slavery, and genocide or voluntarily through migration and immigration.

The concept of diaspora as rooted in dispersal—*the* African diaspora—contrasts with the equally popular notion of Africa *and* its diaspora. Conceptualizing diaspora around the act of dispersal produces theories that are heterogeneous and never fixed in time or space. Fluidity is critical for understanding acts of critical appropriations because in order to be understood as transnational one cannot be fixed in time or space. When speaking about the Black Atlantic, Paul Gilroy notes, "The concept of space is itself transformed when it is seen less through outmoded notions of fixity and place and more in terms of the ex-centric communicative circuitry that has enabled dispersed populations to converse, interact and even synchronise" ("Route Work" 22). The act of privileging syncretism and transculturation over authenticity and origins creates the space for African Americans to be understood as capable of possessing transnational identities and not be bound by a national identity that is tied to one particular place and nation.[14]

The privileging Gilroy speaks of resonates with Stuart Hall when Hall proposes thinking of identity as a "production" that "is never complete, always in process, and always constituted within, not outside, representation" (392). Although Hall privileges the Caribbean and Caribbean people in his often-cited essay, "Cultural Identity and Diaspora," his point about the Americas or the "New World," as he terms it, must necessarily be extended to all peoples who inhabit that space. Thus, his assertion, "It is the space where the creolisations and assimilations and syncretisms were negotiated. . . . The 'New World' presence—America, *Terra Incognita*—is

therefore itself the beginning of diaspora, of diversity, of hybridity and difference" (401), also positions African Americans within his "New World"
discourse that insists upon identity as heterogeneous and always in a state
of production and reproduction.

The texts for this study were selected because they privilege difference
and reproduction and simultaneously interrogate origins and authenticity. Over the past forty years, African American women artists have created a proliferation of cultural products that critique patriarchy and reflect some degree of diaspora consciousness. Toni Morrison's *Tar Baby* and
Paule Marshall's *Praisesong for the Widow,* for example, have become classic representations of such texts. These texts, however, represent community, family, and kinship in homogenous ways that in the process of oblit-
erating heterogeneity also create troubling roles for black women—roles
that impose strength on them by virtue of being both black and female.
In *Tar Baby,* for example, Jadine is critiqued for not fitting an essentialist
notion of black womanhood, which is evidenced by Morrison's insistence,
along with the scholarship on that text, that black women hold things together.[15] Jadine is punished for not being in touch with her "roots" and
failing to hold things together. In a similar fashion, Avey Johnson takes a
journey that leads her back to her "roots," her family and its West African
heritage. Unlike Jadine, however, Avey embraces kinship and community
and is redeemed from her previous waywardness.

This project is interested in texts that call for a paradigm shift that
does not allow for easy returns to primordial sites—the site of the mother
(primordial Africa)—and static epistemologies. The texts analyzed in this
book both complicate notions of sameness and cultural constancy and
consider critically how such notions affect the social and political positions African American women occupy. While there are, of course, other
texts that fit this paradigm, these particular texts speak to one another
in a dialogue about African American women's complex identities and
the problems homogeneity creates in the construction of those identities.
The selected texts ultimately do not draw on international travel as key
to shaping African American women's production of knowledge, though
some do include migration.

Gilroy and Hall have been influential in shaping how scholars con-
ceptualize diaspora. While their attention to difference and heterogene-

ity is important, two significant shortcomings of their theorizations are the privileging of travel—travel in the contemporary moment versus at some point in the past—and the absence of any attention to how gender shapes concepts of the African diaspora. A complexity of African American identity is lost when the African diaspora is conceptualized as being synonymous with movement. The popularity of approaching diaspora as a concept rooted in travel can be seen in Wendy Walters's *At Home in Diaspora* when she constructs diaspora as an experience that is contingent upon geographical displacement; in order to be at home in diaspora, one must first leave home.[16] For the authors Walters examines, home is no longer a generic, primordial space in Africa, but it also is not the initial location of dispersal. Thus, Walters's attention to African American writers is limited to the expatriates Richard Wright and Chester Himes as they look from Europe at the United States as a conflicted home space. In *The Practice of Diaspora*, Brent Hayes Edwards also constructs diaspora as a space that is predicated on movement; travel is inherent in the international alliances between black intellectuals in New York and Paris that frame his project.[17] Both of these concepts of diaspora emphasize movement, which ultimately presents diaspora or diasporaness as bound up in economics, and thus, all too often it becomes an elitist discourse that can only account for the experiences of those who can afford to be mobile and those who can imagine being mobile in the first place.

Walters's and Edwards's texts are pivotal in diaspora literary and cultural studies; yet, these texts fail to register the gendered nature of movement, which is bound up in the gendered nature of diaspora as a concept. Two notable recent diasporic texts that do not privilege international travel and that do attend to the work of black women are Michelle M. Wright's *Becoming Black: Creating Identity in the African Diaspora* and Ifeoma Kiddoe Nwankwo's *Black Cosmopolitanism: Racial Consciousness and Transnational Identity in the Nineteenth-Century Americas*. Wright's comparative theorization of how black intellectuals responded to Enlightenment discourse through nationalist and patriarchal frameworks reflects the level of gender consciousness often missing in diaspora studies. Although Nwankwo does not attend exclusively to black women, and in fact, only includes one black woman, Mary Prince, her theoretical framework shares the most commonalities with how I theorize the transnational. Nwankwo is also interested in how ideas travel and influence the construction of black transnational communities and not necessarily how the people themselves construct transnational identities through travel. *Black Cosmopolitanism* shares similarities with the way that David Luis-Brown theorizes decolonization in *Waves of Decolonization: Discourses of Race and Hemispheric Citizenship in Cuba, Mexico, and the United States* as being bound up in expanding national boundaries. While Nwankwo and Luis-Brown do include women writers and cultural figures in their analysis, they do not use an intersectional approach that pointedly considers how those women's experiences and ideologies are shaped by not only blackness but also by being women.

Numerous black women scholars have attended to the gendered nature of movement, noting that black women travel, but their motivation for travel and their pursuits once elsewhere often differ significantly from black men's travel agendas.[18] Furthermore, their travel is often more localized and restricted to region (the Americas), as opposed to the trans-hemispheric travel performed by artists and scholars like Richard Wright, Chester Himes, and W. E. B. Du Bois, African American men who traveled, and therefore are diasporic, or at least are included in work on the African diaspora. Mary Helen Washington, Deborah McDowell, and Claudia Tate note that "the journey" in black women's writing was often depicted as an internal, psychological journey. Carol Boyce Davies points out, however, "that Black women did travel and that they perhaps negotiated movement in different ways," and as such, "we need to read escape/flight critically against a series of modalities—time, age, space, education, language, ability, family, location and so on" (135). Not acknowledging black women's alternative journeys and overlooking the ways in which their travel is complicated by race, gender, and class places serious limitations on our ability to view black women as diasporic subjects. These differences in mobility limit African American women in particular from being the focus of many diaspora or transnational projects.

A theoretical limitation of diaspora as a concept that frames how people of African descent construct identities is the tendency to fail to attend to women and to those who "stay put," the immobile transnationalists. A more expansive conceptualization of diaspora that considers the significance of staying put just as equally as travel creates the possibility for a radical re-conceptualization of diaspora that takes seriously the experiences and unique predicaments of African American women who through a diaspora consciousness construct transnational identities. This means that writers, intellectuals, and performers like Richard Wright, W. E. B. Du Bois, and Josephine Baker—African Americans who traveled and settled elsewhere—do not trump individuals like Toni Morrison, Kasi Lemmons, and Beyoncé Knowles whose ideas and art are transnational in scope. This is not to say that Morrison, Lemmons, and Knowles have never left the United States, because they have; rather the point is that they return, and home does not become elsewhere for them like it did for Wright, Du Bois, and Baker. Inserting the transnational in discourse on African American women creates a space to reconstruct family and community in ways that fulfill African American women intellectually and socially; the transnational allows them to imagine home spaces right here in the United States.

DISAPPEARING ACTS IN BLACK WOMEN'S STUDIES

A limitation on how diaspora is conceptualized is not the only challenge for African American women living in and producing cultural work in the United States. The emergence of transnational studies as a significant subfield of cultural studies has presented challenges for the field of black studies, and particularly for black women's studies, which flourished during the 1970s and 1980s. Scholars now refer to this period as the Black Women's Literary Renaissance[19] due to the significant production of literature and criticism by black women writers during these decades. Both the academic and popular attention during the renaissance prodded scholar Ann duCille to insist that "the black woman writer is a bonanza," while in the same breath she warns, "[h]istorical amnesia may displace her at any time" (Skin Trade 92). Her warning was prophetic. By the late 1990s and into the twenty-first century, the prominence or at least the attention given to black women's studies dwindled as new discourses—diaspora, transnational, and borderland studies—have demanded a space in cultural studies discourse. The academy, then, is an obvious place to turn to in order to understand the challenges black women's studies faces in the twenty-first century.

Ann duCille laments the lack of respect for the field of black feminist studies in her provocative essay, "The Occult of True Black Womanhood." She is concerned that the field of black feminist studies was not taken seriously as "a discipline with a history and a body of rigorous scholarship underpinning it" and was instead treated "like an anybody-can-play pickup game played on an open field" (95). duCille's lament is echoed in "Whither Black women's studies," an interview Eveylnn M. Hammonds conducts with Beverly Guy-Sheftall in which both women discuss the absence of any prominent black women's studies program(s) in the United States, and Guy-Sheftall adds, "I think it's also fair to say that most well-established African American studies programs do not have even what I would call a serious black women's studies concentration" (66). Guy-Sheftall and duCille make these poignant observations about the neglect of black women's studies during the late 1990s—two decades after Barbara Smith's pivotal essay "Toward a Black Feminist Criticism" laid the groundwork for what would become the field of black feminist criticism/black women's studies on institutional and public levels.

The concern with the state of black women's studies has also manifested in critical reviews that examine scholarship and paradigms that have shaped the last thirty years of black feminist criticism. In "On Waiting to Exhale: Or What To Do When You're Feeling Black and Blue, A Review of Recent Black Feminist Criticism," Sharon Patricia Holland examines how scholarship published during the mid-1990s by Karla F. C. Holloway, Ann duCille, Deborah E. McDowell, Madhu Dubey, and Cheryl A. Wall "[a]ll seek to lay to rest the conflict between legitimate Black feminist inquiry and the 'culture of complaint' often attributed to such inquiry" (102). In her 2007 essay, "That the Mothers May Soar and the Daughters May Know Their Names: A Retrospective of Black Feminist Literary Criticism," Farah Jasmine Griffin lays out a fabulous historical timeline and bibliography of black feminist literary criticism. What this essay lacks, and what even Noliwe M. Rooks's "Like Canaries in the Mines: Black Women's Studies at the Millennium," which proclaims to offer a sense of the field at the millennium, lacks is a critical discussion about future directions in black women's studies/black feminist criticism.

Kimberly Springer, however, does offer some speculation on future directions in "Third Wave Black Feminism?" through an examination of personal narratives by Joan Morgan, Lisa Jones, and Veronica Chambers. Springer's analysis of shifts or "waves" in black feminism delves into ideological and theoretical differences between second-wave and third-wave feminists and concludes with the assertion that black feminist scholars must make feminism more appealing to marginalized groups. Springer's proposal to do this through the use of popular culture recaptures the feminist mantra that the "personal is political." In her response to Springer, Beverly Guy-Sheftall argues that she is not as convinced that young black feminists like Joan Morgan "are carrying on the legacy left by nineteenth-century abolitionists, antilynching crusaders, club women, Civil Rights organizers, Black nationalist revolutionaries, and 1970s Black feminists, though I would like to embrace her argument." Guy-Sheftall believes Morgan has rejected "fundamental feminist principles" that Guy-Sheftall still believes are relevant across generations (1093–94). Guy-Sheftall draws this conclusion after citing several instances in which Morgan proposes that hip-hop feminists are ambivalent about full equality, often willing to make concessions in return for patriarchal forms of chivalry. Perhaps even more disturbing to Guy-Sheftall is Morgan's sense throughout her narrative that the use of sexuality for economic and social gain can indeed be a feminist act. In this regard, Guy-Sheftall makes a valid point about Morgan's brand of feminism because, while Morgan does offer an inviting way for her generation of black women to think about and even embrace feminism, throughout her narrative Morgan fails to consider seriously the shortcomings of a feminism that makes a space for objectification and commodification.

Although the work of each of these scholars articulates concerns within the field of black women's studies differently, inherent in each discussion is an observation that black women's studies is not taken seriously as a discipline. To be further convinced of this, one need only to consider the October 2006 issue of *PMLA* dedicated to Nellie McKay. The issue proposes to account for feminist criticism today; however, except for the interview with McKay, the issue fails to address black feminist criticism. I was sorely disappointed when I read the interview with McKay and saw it was not followed by a critical discussion of black feminist criticism today (McKay's interview focused on the birth of black women's studies in the academy). It would only seem appropriate that in an issue that highlighted the broader focus of "feminist criticism today" and that explicitly identified its intent as one that memorialized a key figure in the shaping of black women's studies that something more would necessarily be said in regard to the field she shaped. Not one of the seven essays following the interview addressed black women's/feminist studies or even feminist issues for women of color in general except for one self-ingratiating article discussing an Anglo-American feminist's pen-pal relationship with an Iraqi feminist scholar. Left to *PMLA* it would seem that issues affecting black women diminished significantly in the twenty-first century.

THE RACIAL IMPLICATIONS OF THE TRANSNATIONAL

Of course issues affecting black women did not diminish in the twenty-first century. The troubled status of women's studies as a marginalized discipline and black women's "precarious and dangerous" position "on the periphery of the already marginalized" (Carby 11) has something to do with black women vanishing. There is, however, a more critical factor that polices black women's studies in the academy: a shift to a post-national paradigm during the late 1990s.[20] This shift creates quite a dilemma for women artists of color in general and for African American women artists in particular. The post-national paradigm demands that how we assess cultural identity be rethought through a transnational and global lens that rejects U.S.-centric scholarship that privileges U.S. exceptionalism. This shift fostered both academic and mass-media acclamations and sometimes celebrations that the significance of race was declining. Reflective of this shift, cultural productions and theoretical frameworks that emphasize nationalism and scholarship invested in "identity politics" become viewed as regressive.[21] In the academic arena it manifests as back-to-feminism-as-usual in *PMLA* where women of color are back in their invisible location on the periphery, or it manifests as the "newfound" interest in issues like feminism and Islam or feminism and borders. Sandra K. Soto offers a compelling analysis of the dangers of placing feminist scholarship on U.S. women of color in contradistinction to transnationalism in her essay, "Where in the Transnational World Are U.S. Women of Color?" Soto points out the irony in that, just when women of color were beginning to find a place in women's studies, a new body of scholarship displaces them once again, conflating them "with the very problems that transnational feminists seek to redress" (122).

The configuration of global versus local that Soto critiques is made more complicated by Karla F. C. Holloway when she argues that the turn to the global not only erases U.S. bodies of color, it also erases white bodies from cultural and political analysis: "Despite significant attention to pluralism in the field . . . contemporary politics of transnationalism have once again buried the bodies of whiteness. . . . U.S. women's studies has disappeared these bodies and their relationship to their color as academic objects of analysis, turning their attention away from the complex politics of U.S. gendered whiteness" (3, 6). The disappearance of gendered whiteness that Holloway critiques is bound up in the post-national discourse that espouses a need to abandon racialized identity politics, espousals that fail to think critically about the intricate relationship between race and gender. Susan Gubar in "What Ails Feminist Criticism" affirms the suspicious nature of the embrace of transnationalism by women's studies that Holloway addresses. Gubar demonizes racialized identity politics and poststructuralism, asserting they are dis-eases that are strangling the life out of women's studies. She complains: "I could call the problem a bad case of critical anorexia, for racialized identity politics made the word *women* slim down to stand only for a very particularized kind of woman, whereas poststructuralists obliged the term to disappear altogether" (901). Gubar's "captivity" narrative, as Rey Chow refers to it, (re) positions white women as victims, a status that is resented in third-wave discourse and at times used to demonize second-wave politics. Robyn Wiegman also responds to Gubar's critique, asserting that, through Gubar's effort to explain the shift from critiques of patriarchal masculinism to internal struggles within feminism, Gubar represents feminism's transition from civic spaces to the university as an unfortunate journey in which "feminism lost its way, traveling through theoretical 'darkness' as women of color and poststructuralists took *women* hostage" (365).

A critical transition in feminist criticism develops from 1998 when Gubar publishes her essay and 2007 when Holloway publishes hers. The serious discomfort that Gubar experiences with attention to "local" color—what she describes as a dis-ease—has been cured by transnational discourse, because transnationalism not only shifts attention away from local color, but it also shifts attention from the critiques of local white-ness that Gubar finds to be "divisive" politics that lead to the "suicide" of women's studies. According to scholars like Holloway and Soto, the turn to transnationalism in women's studies becomes an "escape hatch" for some white feminists that either allows them to "re-claim" the field or at the very least to turn their attention to international debates that allow them not to feel as uncomfortable about their white privilege.

To be fair, although the transition to transnationalism in women's studies demonstrates some serious concerns in regard to U.S. racialized bodies, the slow incorporation of women of color in women's studies de-partments and the emergence of third-wave feminist discourse in the 1990s suggest some progress. The doctoral-granting women's studies pro-grams have made a notable effort to recruit and hire women- (and some-times men-) of-color faculty, as have some smaller non-graduate-degree-granting programs. A notable case is my academic institution, The Ohio State University, whose women's studies doctoral program was created under the leadership of its former chair, Valerie Lee, an African American woman. Her leadership was also instrumental in the hiring of faculty of color and the creation of courses attending to women of color in that de-partment (as well as in the English Department, which she later chaired). The recognition by women's studies programs that they need to have courses that attend to racial differences as well as the bodies that repre-sent those differences surely is influenced by the centrality of women of color in third-wave feminist discourse.

In contrast to what Astrid Henry refers to as the often "overly simplis-tic and dogmatic" perception of second-wave feminist politics, third-wave feminist politics tends to embrace complexity, ambiguity, and pluralities (150). Rebecca Walker, daughter of Alice Walker, coined the term "third wave feminist" in her 1992 *Ms.* article, "Becoming the Third Wave," that responded to the Clarence Thomas hearings. Walker later edited a col-lection of essays, *To Be Real: Telling the Truth and Changing the Face of Feminism* (1995), largely penned by women and men of color who ex-plore ways to rethink feminist politics and to articulate how the personal is political in their lives and activism. Another influential collection that takes an intersectional approach to contemporary feminism and where and how women of color are situated in it is Daisy Hernández and Bushra

Rehman's *Colonize This! Young Women of Color on Today's Feminism*. When analyzing the centrality of anthologies like those listed above to third-wave feminism, Henry explains that, while "third-wave feminism is frequently presented as a racially and ethnically diverse movement, with black women moved from the margin to the center of this new wave . . . the popular media's seeming inability to acknowledge feminism as anything other than a white middle–class movement has created a fairly whitewashed representation of the third wave" (163). Henry also notes the failure of the mainstream media to recognize that the Thomas hearings catalyzed the movement, a movement in which black women played a critical role in developing. My analyses attempt to "tell the truth" about the erasures and invisibilities that African American women experience in women's studies, black and diaspora studies, and transnational studies. My goal is to demonstrate the complexities of the lives and experiences of African American women in the United States that produce transnational identities in order to add insight to how scholars theorize race, gender, and transnationalism.

Critical Appropriations is comprised of three parts that identify a variety of critical appropriations in African American women's contemporary cultural productions and consider how those acts respond to marginalized positions they occupy in interdisciplinary fields. Part One, "Toward a Critical Gender Consciousness," considers the intersections of race and gender when diasporic theories of cultural identity are privileged. The two chapters in Part One focus specifically on the type of transnational homes that are being built and the challenge of creating safe spaces for black women in those homes. Chapter 1 analyzes how the Convent women in *Paradise* are rescued from the holds of the colonial and imperial politics of the nation-state when they embrace the syncretic blend of spiritual and cultural knowledge that they discover while living at the Convent. I approach this novel by reading the affair between Consolata Sosa and Deacon Morgan through the trope of incest. The affair represents an act of cultural cannibalism that is infused with principles of Vodou. The metaphorical incest that frames the affair produces a "self-love ethic" that the Convent women embrace through an initiation process that closely resembles the Afro-Brazilian religion Candomblé. The "self-love ethic" enables the Convent women to embrace transnational identities, to metaphysically cross borders and dwell in a suspended, in-between space. Negotiating immobile, transnational identities bestows grace upon the Convent women, but the price for being released from mental and physical restraints is death. Chapter 2 examines how anthropology is positioned in Erna Brodber's *Louisiana* as a site of empowerment for people of African descent. I do this by proposing that in *Louisiana* a palimpsest narrative emerges in which the life and experiences of the protagonist, Ella Townsend Kohl, signifies on and memorializes the life and work of Floridian anthropologist, folklorist, and writer Zora Neale Hurston. A close examination of this narrative identifies trans-historical challenges with community and gender that black women have faced when attempting to position themselves in black/diaspora studies. Analysis of the palimpsest narrative that Brodber creates when Ella's life and experiences are written over those of Zora Neal Hurston is critical for understanding how the intersection of blackness and femaleness creates unique challenges for identity formation as this text, too, ends in death.

Part Two, "Popular Culture, Transnational Feminism, and the Limits of Sisterhood," examines how tropes of sisterhood are employed when efforts to achieve a critical gender consciousness fail. Using the musical and video productions of Beyoncé Knowles as example, this section focuses on how African American women grapple with the promises and limitations of a transnational identity by centering popular culture as a fruitful site to examine the community and home space that is built on transnational sisterhood. In chapter 3, I focus on Beyoncé's *B'Day* disc that was released in 2006, and particularly the re-release of that disc in 2007 with Spanish songs and the release of the "Beautiful Liar" music video collaboration with Latina pop icon Shakira, an act of critical appropriation that Beyoncé hopes will situate her and her work as not simply African American, but as transnational. This chapter considers the challenges surrounding African American women's collaboration and marketing in the hip-hop music industry as a catalyst for the *B'Day* disc, Beyoncé's rather ingenious collaborations on the disc and the music video, and whether there are risks when transnational sisterhoods are formed without a praxis framed by a critical gender consciousness.

The ending of chapter 3 provides a segue into the third part of the book, "Third Wave Feminism, Paradigm Shifts, and Black Masculinity," which is positioned as a rejoinder to Parts One and Two. These chapters explore texts that I identify as resisting the privileging of diasporic theories of cultural identity and instead function as examples of the value in deconstructing and interrogating the risks and benefits of such privileging. Furthermore, the two chapters in this section focus on a different kind of gender dynamic than the text in Part Two. Instead of attending to the strength and limitations of sisterhood, these chapters consider the possible challenges inherent in heterosexual, intra-racial gender dynamics.

Chapter 4 considers how critical appropriations of *Brasilidade* (Brazilianness) in Danzy Senna's *Caucasia* operate as a warning about the potential pitfalls of uncritical appropriations. The approach I use for analyzing the pitfalls is an examination of the father-daughter relationship in the novel and the silence that surrounds it. Although my analysis focuses primarily on *Caucasia*, I draw on Gayl Jones's *Corregidora* in order to consider how the false propaganda of racial democracy and black incorporation into the nation that was perpetuated by Brazilianness rhetoric extended across hemispheres to the African American imagination in the United States. I argue that such propaganda produces a metaphorical aphasia in the fathers in both *Caucasia* and *Corregidora*. In an act that perhaps responds to the troubles produced by privileging Brazilianness rhetoric in *Corregidora*, *Caucasia* examines this appropriation and offers an insightful paradigm shift around notions of family, kinship, and community that produces a transnational narrative without privileging travel while also avoiding death and sisterhood as the only routes for African American women embracing transnational identities.

I conclude with chapter 5, returning to the trope of incest. The trope in Kasi Lemmons's *Eve's Bayou* emphasizes the cultural hybridity inherent in the United States, while also warning viewers of the stasis that can be produced as a result of immobility. Incest acts as a signifier of U.S. imperialism, revealing the transnational matters that are unique to people who dwell in a nation within a nation. By setting the film in Louisiana and utilizing the trope of incest to frame the narrative, Lemmons signifies heavily on the historical memory that is inscribed within that geography, especially through William Faulkner's *Go Down, Moses*. If viewers consider incest in this film as a signifier of the racial residue inherent in Faulkner's text instead of focusing on the apparently titillating possibility of molestation that many critics and viewers are enraptured by, then incest becomes no more than parody. *Eve's Bayou* appropriates theories of hybridity in order to create a counter-narrative about both African American women and African American men's experiences with race, gender, memory, and geography in the United States.

In the epilogue I discuss how moving outside of familiar home spaces is the primary impetus for appropriating diasporic theories of cultural identity. I draw on Saidiya Hartman's memoir *Lose Your Mother: A Journey Along the Atlantic Slave Route* in order to think about how paradigm shifts in these contemporary cultural products rely on critically rethinking notions of kinship, community, and home as key to transnational identity formation.

My attention to transnationalism in black women's studies focuses exclusively on African American women artists and how their cultural products can be understood as transnational. These cultural productions demonstrate transnational sensibilities that critically engage the precarious marginal positions that African American women, their art, and their scholarship are often forced to occupy in the post-national era. *Critical Appropriations* is ultimately invested in how acts of agency and the insistence upon truth telling can both limit and create possibilities when black women artists interrogate their own positions and the value of their work in a racialized global economy. The benefit of identifying critical appropriations of diasporic theories of cultural identity in these productions is that it helps erode confining, geographical, and intellectual boundaries that pigeonhole African Americans in localized and static spaces.

PART ONE

TOWARD A CRITICAL GENDER CONSCIOUSNESS

CHAPTER 1

When Home Is Paradise

Appropriating Acts in Toni Morrison's *Paradise*

P aradise is a migration narrative about two communities, the 8-rocks of Ruby and "stray" women at the Convent, who inadvertently find home spaces in rural Oklahoma. The residents of Ruby are descendants of a proud group of ex-slaves who migrate west from Louisiana and Mississippi after the failure of Reconstruction. As they migrate, each black town they arrive at declares them too poor and too black, "disallowing" them residence. Rather than accept the class and color prejudices as a defeat, the 8-rock clan embraces their blackness as a sign of purity and superiority, literally naming themselves 8-rock, "An abbreviation for eight-rock, a deep deep level in the coal mines" (Morrison, *Paradise* 193). The Convent was originally an "embezzler's folly" and later a Catholic "school" for Arapaho Indian girls before becoming a refuge for four abused and scared young women—Mavis, Gigi, Seneca and Pallas—and a mother-figure, Consolata Sosa, who was kidnapped from Brazil by the former nuns who inhabited the Convent. In spite of the fact that both communities seek refuge in rural Oklahoma, the 8-rock residents and the Convent women are deeply divided ideologically, a division that ultimately leads to the slaughter that opens the first page of the novel. Juxtaposing the 1976 massacre of the Convent women with the U.S. Bicentennial as the setting of the opening of the novel, the remainder of the narrative is a non-linear recounting of each Convent woman's story and a recounting of the stories of several 8-rock families, particularly the Morgan family, that culminates with the planning of the massacre and the events immediately following the incident. Much of the literary criticism on *Paradise* has interpreted the novel as being situated in a nationalist paradigm that critiques the limits of citizenship, gender, and violence. By identifying a variety of critical appropriations of diasporic cultural theories, a transnational narrative emerges that offers a more nuanced understanding of how nation, gender, and violence work together to create a space for the Convent women who, to borrow from Wendy Walters, seek to "be at home in diaspora."[1]

Recognizing an intricate relationship between nation, gender, and violence in *Paradise* is critical for conducting an analysis that shifts the paradigm from national to transnational. When Lone DuPres encourages Consolata to use her gift of "stepping in," Consolata resists, insisting that she does not believe in magic and, no doubt, recalls Mary Magna's warning, "But be very careful . . . I think she practices." Knowing that Consolata felt "that the church and everything holy forbade its claims to knowingness and its practice," Lone simply responds to Consolata's resistance to her alternative way of knowing by noting, "Sometimes folks need more" (244). For the Convent women, the practice of appropriating diasporic theories of cultural identity is a response to Lone's notion of "needing more"— more than the failed democratic promises of the nation and more than the limited forms of knowledge that Catholicism and Protestantism have provided them. Through a hybrid blend of belief systems, representing Africa, Europe, the Americas and spanning ancient and modern periods, critical appropriations provide the Convent women with an alternative to the sense of homelessness and unbelonging they felt in the disparate U.S. geographies they inhabited prior to arriving at the Convent.

Critical appropriations are not just about having a "homing desire" and "feeling at home" in diaspora when home is located elsewhere, as Avtar Brah has discussed in relation to migrant diaspora subjects in *Cartographies of Diaspora: Contesting Identities*. Critical appropriations are about both "feeling at home" and locating home right where one happens to be. Such activities rely heavily on both the imagination and on openness to new forms of knowledge. In the case of African Americans this is particularly important because it not only provides a way to negotiate exclusions from democratic ideals, but also to negotiate the exclusions from being understood as diasporic subjects when they chose to stay put and lay claims to a new homeland, the United States. When African Americans appropriate cultural theories that are formulated with transnational properties, their act of appropriation enables them to embrace transnational identities.

Appropriating acts in *Paradise* and the ideologies that shape them share similarities with two cultural and literary manifestos produced in the Americas during the twentieth century. Oswald de Andrade's 1928 "Cannibalist Manifesto"[2] acts as what Leslie Bary refers to "as a paradigm for the creation of a modern and cosmopolitan, but still authentically national culture" (35). In the manifesto, Andrade emphasizes that, in the formation of a national identity, European culture should not be rejected but instead "devoured," incorporating its strengths with those of the native self. The same year that Oswald de Andrade published the "Cannibalist Manifesto," Mário de Andrade published *Macunaíma*, a narrative that has become a classic Brazilian literary-folkloric text that reflects Oswald de Andrade' s public declaration about the relationship between the modern, the cosmopolitan, and the authentic. *Macunaíma* addresses both the search for a national identity in a multiethnic and multicultural nation as well as how technological change affects the formation of a national identity. Cultural diversity and technological change create problems for 8-rock notions of racial purity in *Paradise*.

Three Martinican writers and intellectuals— Jean Bernabé, Patrick Chamoiseau, and Raphaël Confiant—wrote *In Praise of Creoleness* in 1989.[3] Like Oswald and Mário de Andrade, these writers are concerned with how Martinicans in particular, but Caribbean people in general, forge a national/regional and cultural identity that is divorced from colonial ties with Europe. The literary movement known as *Créolité* or "Creoleness" privileges linguistic, racial, and cultural hybridity in order to encourage Caribbean people to embrace an organic identity produced in the contact zones of the Americas rather than looking to colonial powers like France or "lost" homelands like Africa when forging a cultural identity. The Convent women are rescued from the holds of the colonial and imperial politics of the nation-state when they embrace the syncretic blend of spiritual and cultural knowledge that they discover while living at the Convent.

Paradise operates in the same vein as these two manifestos. Through a juxtaposition of the Convent women and the 8-rock, *Paradise* proposes

an identity for African Americans that is rooted in hybridity and is localized in the Americas rather than a lost homeland. The Creoleness and
cultural cannibalism in *Paradise* is represented through critical appropriations of Vodou, Candomblé, and the doctrine from the Gnostic text, the
Nag Hamadi.

I begin my analysis with the brief affair of Consolata Sosa and Deacon Morgan, the "weaker" of the Morgan twins, explaining how reading the affair through the trope of incest reveals two specific critical appropriations: the cultural cannibalism embraced by Brazilian *modernistos*
and the principles of Vodou. Cultural cannibalism or *anthropophagia*
and Vodou work together to produce a "self-love ethic" that the Convent
women embrace through an initiation process that closely resembles the
Afro-Brazilian religion, Candomblé. When Consolata instructs the Convent women how to weave together syncretic, diasporic epistemologies—
Vodou and Candomblé—the Convent women figuratively, and perhaps
later literally, rebirth themselves in ways that make them comfortable
"down here in Paradise" (*Paradise* 318). As the Convent women learn from
Consolata and as Richard Misner, Ruby's Baptist minister from outside
the community, hopes his "love" sermon teaches Ruby, love is central to
being at home in diaspora. Love is critical to accepting one's self as hybrid
and to registering a sense of belonging that is neither isolated like Ruby
nor elsewhere like the Ruby teenagers' romantic notions of Africa or the
unknown places of refuge the Convent women were all running to. The
lesson on love is presented in two forms. What I refer to as "visitors" assist certain female characters in navigating the path of self-love.[4] Soane
and Dovey Morgan, sisters and wives of the Morgan twin patriarchs, and
Consolata all encounter visitors, but Consolata is the only woman who
actually acts upon the knowledge her visitor brings. The ways in which
Morrison signifies on a particular book of the Nag Hamadi is instrumental for understanding why Consolata is able to discern and respond to the
knowledge her visitor brings. The "self-love ethic" manifests through the
appropriation of Vodou and Candomblé and, by embracing visitors and
the Nag Hamadi, the Convent women are able to be at home in diaspora.
Both feeling at home and locating home in *Paradise* is an act of grace that
frees the Convent women from ways of knowing that are narrow, stifling,
and ultimately deadly.

IN SEARCH OF A HOME SPACE

Grace, or Gigi as she is called throughout most of the narrative, is the only long-term Convent resident who arrives in Ruby, Oklahoma, intentionally. She is in search of entwined trees and rhubarb pie after a failed search for stone copulating figures in Wish, Arizona. Gigi begins her journey toward the Convent after, along with her boyfriend, witnessing the shooting of a young black boy during a civil rights protest. The investment that Gigi has in the intimacy and reproduction inherent in the copulating stone figures and entwined branches is informed by the failures of U.S. democracy to protect its African American citizens from violence and disenfranchisement, as well as its failure to regard them as full citizens. Gigi, therefore, does not just end up at the Convent because she is searching for entwined branches and rhubarb pie; she ends up at the Convent because she is desperately searching for solace from a tumultuous U.S. racial climate. The copulating rock formation and entwined trees represent Gigi's attempt to come to terms with her sense of dislocation. They are expressive of her efforts to locate a space in which she can both feel at home and be at home in the United States; Gigi ultimately seeks a freely given love or *grace*.

While Gigi's search functions as a metaphor for a larger national narrative of incorporation and belonging, the affair between Consolata and Deacon operates as a transnational metaphor for diasporic belonging. As a child, Consolata Sosa was kidnapped from her Brazilian home by U.S. nuns and brought to Oklahoma, where she spent the rest of her life isolated from the outside world and indentured to the nuns. At forty years of age, Consolata briefly rebels against the isolation and celibacy imposed by the nuns and has an affair with Deacon Morgan, the "weaker" of the Morgan twins, the power-wielding patriarchs of Ruby. For Consolata, the affair represents a way to return to the folk life and racial confraternity of her homeland—an Afro-Brazilian home whose music, language, food, and culture are a syncretic blend of Africa, Europe, and the Americas. The entwined trees that promise grace to Gigi also represent grace for Consolata, as the trees, unlike the copulating rocks, do indeed exist at the site of Consolata's and Deacon's rendezvous. Just as the trees are a marker of longing for Gigi, Consolata also registers both feeling at home and being at home when copulating at the foot of those trees. Both the trees and Deacon reconnect Consolata to her Afro-Brazilian roots.[5] Through the literal body of Deacon Morgan, Consolata believes that she has located a space that is, in Morrison's words, "snug and wide open" ("Home" 9), a space consummated at the foot of "two fig trees growing into each other" (*Paradise* 230). Consolata fails to note, however, that the trees will grow, but they will not bear fruit, which is similar to the smaller family sizes and dying children that threaten the future of Ruby—a population and reproduction problem that Ruby emphatically blames on the Convent women.

Even before her affair with Deacon, Consolata believed there was an innate sameness between her and the Ruby residents. When accompanying Mary Magna on the seventeen-mile trip to Ruby to purchase pharmacy supplies, Consolata senses "Something unbridled was going on under the scalding sun." Consolata and Mary Magna arrive during the infamous derby race that dubbed Steward and Deacon's nephew "K.D." because he rode his horse and won the race as if he were competing in the Kentucky Derby. It is at the moment of K.D.'s victory that Consolata hears the faint "Sha sha sha. Sha sha sha," sounds that represent her erotic and communal desire for Deacon and Ruby. These sounds are followed by "a memory of just such skin and just such men, dancing with women in the streets to music beating like an infuriated heart, torsos still, hips making small circles above legs moving so rapidly it was fruitless to decipher how such ease was possible." Although these men were laughing and running instead of dancing, and living in a hamlet rather than "a loud city full of glittering black people, Consolata knew she knew them" (226). Consolata's attraction to Deacon is not simply erotic, but laden with a memory of a cultural past that she wants to return to.

When considered together, Gigi's search and Consolata's and Deacon's affair operate as metaphors for love and belonging that haunt many post–civil rights African American communities. The repeating desire of the characters in *Paradise* to locate home leads literary scholar Susan Strehle to conclude, "*Paradise* wonders whether African American people can find or make a home in America, whether its history of racism can ever yield to a nonracist and psychically safe space" (34). The search for home and safety leaves Gigi and Consolata needing "more." When Gigi's boyfriend does not show up at their rendezvous site after his arrest and jail stint as a result of the race riot, Gigi gives up, "Reluctantly. The eternal desert coupling, however, she held on to for dear and precious life. Underneath gripping dreams of social justice, of an honest people's guard—more powerful than her memory of the boy spitting blood into his hands—the desert lovers broke her heart (*Paradise* 64).

Consolata shares a similar moment of disappointment when the sense of home and sameness that Deacon restores to her is terminated almost simultaneously by Deacon's omniscient twin, Steward, and Consolata's disturbing act of biting Deacon's lip. Consolata and Deacon's relationship changes irrevocably when she invites him to her house: "There is a small room in the cellar. . . . I will fix it, make it beautiful. With candles. It's cool and dark in the summer, warm as coffee in winter. We'll have a lamp to see each other with, but nobody can see us. We can shout as loud as we want and nobody can hear. Pears are down there and walls of wine . . . do it' she urges him. 'Please do it. Come to my house'" (237). As Deacon ponders her invitation, Consolata bites his lip, and hums over the blood she licks from his lip. The humming and licking, more so than the biting itself, repulse and scare Deacon. "He'd sucked air sharply. Said, 'Don't ever do that again.' But his eyes, first startled, then revolted, had said . . . who would chance pears and a wall of prisoner wine with a woman bent on eating him like a meal?" (239).[6]

When Consolata bites Deacon's lip, it is not the pain that troubles him. Deacon is troubled by how the lip biting and blood licking are anthropophagic acts of incorporation. Although Consolata does not view Deacon as an enemy, she does understand him as having something of value to her—blackness, both physically and culturally—that she wants to incorporate into herself. Deacon's blackness functions as a sort of Freudian lost love object for Consolata. Deacon, however, is appalled by her act of violation because it awakens him to his breaking of every unwritten rule of Ruby that the forefathers declared: no scattering (leaving Ruby); no adultery; and a maintaining of racial purity. The rule about maintaining racial purity—8-rockness—in particular terrifies Deacon because he does not understand Consolata, a racially hybrid woman, as sharing a kinship with him. Despite being displaced from her homeland and culture for thirty years, Consolata not only remembers that home and culture when she encounters Ruby residents, but she also mourns the loss. Consolata is driven by this longing when she naively and, perhaps, unconsciously attempts to regain the feeling of kinship that she lost in her dislocation by biting Deacon's lip and licking the blood. When Deacon reacts with disdain, Consolata bemoans the loss of her connector to her cultural roots when she admits, "'Dear Lord, I didn't want to eat him. I just wanted to go *home*'" (240, emphasis mine).

Consolata's belief that she shares a sameness with Deacon and by extension Ruby culminates in a love-struckness that takes on an "edible quality," which Consolata attributes to the thirty years of celibacy after the "dirty pokings her ninth year subjected her to" (228). The edible quality of her love-struckness is much more complicated than simply being a response to rape. When Mary Magna scolds Consolata to forget the man that led her astray, Consolata wants to respond, "Sha sha sha. Sha sha sha, she wanted to say, meaning, he and I are the same" (241). Consolata sees no difference between the African Americans in Ruby and the Afro-Brazilians she remembers dancing in the streets of her homeland. For this reason, she believes that, by doing what she perceives to be reestablishing a kinship with Ruby through Deacon, she can in fact return to the past and feel at home.

While Consolata wants to retrieve the ancestral past, Deacon steadfastly works to escape it, and if possible, erase it. Deacon registers no "Sha sha sha" for Consolata or the historical or ancestral past that she invokes. Deacon's interpretation of Consolata's biting and blood licking is driven by a fear of contamination and abhorrence of heterogeneity. Just prior to the Convent ambush, Deacon remembers Consolata as "an uncontrollable, gnawing woman who had bitten his lip just to lap the blood it shed; a beautiful, gold-skinned, outside woman with moss-green eyes that tried to trap a man, close him up in a cellar room with liquor to enfeeble him so they could do carnal things, unnatural things in the dark; a Salomé from whom he had escaped just in time or she would have had his head on a dinner plate. That ravenous ground-fucking woman . . ." (279–80). Deacon fears Consolata because she and the lip biting represent a racial and cultural contamination of the isolating boundaries that Ruby perceives as utopian.

In Deacon's emphatic rejection of an African ancestral past, he also rejects any notion of an African or diasporic identity. Deacon would never believe that he and Consolata, a racially mixed Brazilian woman, share any sameness. For Deacon, Consolata represents the threatening "other" who destroys boundaries.[7] Her lip biting was not simply sexual foreplay, rather it reflected her desire to reproduce her [mixed-race] self, and also a dangerous, covenant-breaking reproduction that Steward fears, "How off the course Deek slid when he was looking in those poison and poisoning eyes . . . and just suppose the hussy had gotten pregnant? Had a mixed-up child? Steward seethed at the thought of that barely averted betrayal of all they owed and promised the Old Fathers" (279). Steward is referencing the Old Fathers' law of "continuance and multiplication," a law that Patricia Best, the unofficial and unwelcome Ruby historian, describes as a deal that Zechariah Morgan (Steward's and Deacon's grandfather who is also known as Coffee and Big Papa) made with God. The deal was that, if Ruby followed the basic commandments of not committing adultery, keeping their bloodline "pure," and maintaining residence in Ruby or not "scattering," they would receive immortality in return (217, 279). "In that case," Pat concludes, "everything that worries them must come from women" (217).

Literary critic Erik Dussere notes that women who transgress "the law" are particularly dangerous because it is through them that racial purity is lost. In regard to Ruby specifically, Dussere acknowledges, "The community's racially pure wholeness is built upon the fear and abhorrence of female sexuality; in order to regulate the exchange of blood, women must be excluded or brought into the circle of incest" (106). Thus, Deacon's and Steward's sentiments toward Consolata coupled with Zechariah's deal echo a national social, historical, literary, and legal narrative that conflates miscegenation and incest in order to maintain white supremacy, or in this case, 8-rock black supremacy.

INCEST AS HOME

The urge to conflate miscegenation and incest against a literary, historical, and legal paradigm of racial supremacy and fear is explored by Werner Sollors in *Neither Black Nor White Yet Both: Thematic Representations of Interracial Literature*. Sollors presents a remarkable in-depth analysis of this urge largely through close readings of a broad spectrum of nineteenth-century literary texts. While the textual analysis is tangential here, several of the points Sollors makes as well as his conclusion are relevant to understanding Deacon's fear and contempt for Consolata. From a legal aspect, Sollors notes, "Charles W. Chesnutt reported that the Mississippi law of 1880 prohibiting miscegenation called interracial marriages 'incestuous and void,'" and that an article in the constitution of Mississippi, repealed in 1987, also decreed that "the marriage of a white person with a Negro or mulatto, or person who shall have one-eighth or more of Negro blood, shall be unlawful and void" (299, 315).[8] Sollors offers two primary explanations for these juridical decrees. The first explanation is that, within the U.S. slave "system of maternal descent that sustains hereditary slavery and the patriarchal belief that kinship is established through the father," there arose a significant reality that unknown miscegenation could lead to unknowingly committing incest (316–18). Slave masters' forced sexual relations with enslaved women created the imminent danger of incest between the slave masters' legitimate and illegitimate offspring. The second explanation is one of catachresis, the rhetorical confusion of one word for another. In the latter case it was a problem of confusing "intermarriage" with "incestuous marriage," intermarriage being marriages that "deviate from endogamous norms"—in other words, marrying outside of the clan or group.

Due to the social non-conformity, intermarriage is commonly condemned as taboo behavior, like incestuous marriage and, thus, the two become conflated (315). Factoring *race* into this rhetorical scenario, however, calls for a consideration of how the conflation of miscegenation, a made-up term to denote racial mixture, and incest is much more than simply a rhetorical fallacy.[9] Sollors insists that miscegenation is a critical fear for any "radical ethnocentrist," and "The paradoxical equation, 'amalgamation is incest,' was set up not in the hope of discovering a human law, but in order to make hybridism seem as 'heinous' as incest" (320).

The conflation of miscegenation and incest, and the horror that miscegenation symbolized for a white supremacist nation, provide a provocative, paradoxical template for reading Deacon's consternation surrounding the lip biting and Steward's fear of hybridity. Debra J. Rosenthal explains that racial hybridity threatens white supremacy because racial mixture "threatens to dissolve difference, represents a loss or destabilization of identity," which creates anxiety around the female body because "women's bodies bear the evidence of miscegenation, with race literalized as a woman's 'issue'" (10–11). Deacon's perception that Consolata desires to re-produce her visibly mixed-race self, as well as the possibility of her and Deacon's sexual encounters resulting in a biological reproduction, threaten to effectively dissolve the racial "purity" Ruby understood was granted to them in their 8-rock deal with God: no adultery; no scattering; and no racial mixing. These are the unwritten laws that the Morgans believe seal their deal of immortality. Not only does Consolata represent "the dung" Ruby left behind, she also threatens to break every law Ruby lives by.

The paradox here is that Ruby is the embodiment of incestuous relationships. While the residents of Ruby might not commit adultery, they inevitably are steeped in incest. Ruby's population is composed of nine large intact families: Blackhorse, Morgan, Poole, Fleetwood, Beauchamp, Cato, Flood, and both DuPres families. In order to maintain their supposed racial purity, they marry each other. There is a hint of this incest in the first half of the text when readers learn that Dovey and Soane are sisters and sister-in-laws. Since there is no blood mixture, the doubleness of their relationship might not seem troubling. Richard Misner notes something peculiar about the Morgan twins: "They performed as one man, but something in Deek's manner made Misner wonder if he wasn't covering for his brother—propping him the way you would a slow-learning child" (62). The suggestion that Steward is propped like "a slow-learning child" could speak to Dovey's multiple miscarriages, which could ultimately be attributed to the genetic deficiencies and sterility common with incest.

In the chapter titled, "Patricia," it becomes clear that the gossip, information, and secrets that parents complain Pat Best is asking their children to divulge is about more than just maintaining one's privacy. In her would-be historical record Pat notes that the Morgans are not as prolific as they once were: "There wasn't much space beneath the K.D.-Arnette entry, but she thought they probably wouldn't need more. If it lived, the baby they were expecting would certainly be an only child. Arnette's mother had only two children, one of whom had fathered only defectives. In addition, these later Morgans were not as prolific as the earlier ones" (191). She also notes a connection between "scattering" and fertility: "Elder [Morgan] died leaving his wife, Susannah (Smith) Morgan,[10] with six children—all of whom moved from Haven to northern states. Zechariah would have hated that. Moving would have been 'scattering' to him. And he was right, for sure enough, from then on the fertility shriveled, even while the bounty multiplied. The more money, the fewer children; the fewer children, the more money to give the fewer children" (193). Nathan DuPres and Mirth Morgan DuPres lost all of their children in a tornado in 1922, and like her parents, Pat has only one child. These three families alone reflect a decreasing fertility.

Ruby's incestuous behavior plays out as a "royal incest," particularly through the attempts by the Morgans to produce more money and to control the financial and social lives of their neighbors. "Royal incest" is certainly a more comforting way of understanding a behavior that holds such a strong social taboo than to recognize its eugenic nature. It is not thoroughly comforting for Pat, however, whose discomfort registers most emphatically when, after a nearly page-and-a half litany of intermarriage and ultimately incestuous marriages, she ends at the Poole family, acknowledging, "But two others of those thirteen children Billie Delia is in love with, and there is something wrong with that but other than number and the blood rules I can't figure out what" (197). Despite Pat's feelings of exclusion based on her father breaking the 8-rock law and marrying a light-skinned woman from outside the community, she remains an 8-rock nonetheless. Her inability to fully recognize the inherent problem in Ruby's social relations lends credence to Sollors's notion that, "After all, the notion of racial 'purity' has an incestuous valence and is based on a program for the future. . . . This position implies that since miscegenation must be avoided at all cost, incest (racially enlarged) becomes an ideal almost by necessity" (322).

Ruby's ideology creates allusions to a reversed notion of Charles W. Chesnutt's "future American." In "The Future American: A Complete Race-Amalgamation Likely to Occur" (1900), Chesnutt presents a utopian illusion that privileges amalgamation. Chesnutt believed that the social and economic progress of black Americans depended upon amalgamation and that amalgamation could be effectively hastened through U.S. imperialism: "The adding to our territories of large areas populated by dark races, some of them already liberally endowed with Negro blood, will en-

hance the relative importance of the non-Caucasian elements of the population, and largely increase the flow of dark blood to the white race, until
the time shall come when distinctions of color shall lose their importance, which will be but the prelude to a complete racial fusion" (135).[11]

Jean Toomer expresses similar sentiments toward race and mixture in
his poem "The Blue Meridian" (1936). Toomer insists that he is a member
of the American race, and he refuses to privilege any one of his "blood-
lines." Stephanie L. Hawkins notes that, in his poem, Toomer describes
the blue race as a hybrid composition of African, Anglo-Saxon, and
American Indian races—a composition that advocates a "deliberate racial
blending . . . as a means to transcend the boundaries of race ideology and
fulfill evolutionary progress toward human perfection" (150). Both Chesnutt and Toomer's ideologies privilege the construction of an identity
based on racial mixture (much like the Brazilian *modernistos*), which is
likely a biased position given both men's near-white phenotypes; nonetheless, it is a privileging that stands at odds with Ruby's racial purity dogma.

Ruby's steadfast compliance with the reversed "Future American"
model—a model advocating racial purity—is complicated further because, in spite of their "royal" incest, the text suggests that Ruby itself has
an indigenous heritage that is reflected in the Black-horse name and the
straight, heavy, black hair that never seems to get absorbed by the 8-rock
blackness. Pat Best reflects that she ". . . married Billy Cato partly because
he was beautiful, partly because he made me laugh, and partly (mostly?)
because he had the midnight skin of the Catos and the Blackhorses,
along with that Blackhorse feature of stick-straight hair. Like Soane's and
Dovey's hair, and like Easter and Scout had" (198–99). This possible prevailing indigenous presence must necessarily be ignored by the 8-rock
because Ruby shares the reversed sentiment of white supremacy's twisted
relationship with incest; Ruby fears that its racial purity will deteriorate
due to racial mixing. Their perceived racial superiority is all they have left
in a nation that says you are not good enough to be fully incorporated citizens, a nation in which the racially marginalized work incessantly to find
a way to transfer their marginalization onto someone else.

Ruby's and especially Deacon's desire for racial purity represents a
paranoia in which miscegenation is a "reminder[s] of repressed, forbidden motives" (Sollors 322). Werner Sollors explains, "Looked at another

way, incest—real or symbolic—may be a *prerequisite* for anything like 'racial purity' or 'race' to emerge. Hence racial fantasies may on the first
level express horror at miscegenation as if it were incest, but on a second
level reveal a deep and necessary yearning for incest" (322). This deep
and necessary yearning materializes when during his wedding ceremony
K.D. dotes on "that Gigi bitch" whom "he had loved for years, an aching
humiliating, self-loathing love that drifted from pining to stealth" (*Paradise* 147). In spite of not being identified as racially mixed, Gigi clearly is
not an 8-rock and therefore does not possess a "pure" blackness like Ruby.
Like his nephew, Deacon is infatuated yet repulsed by Consolata's racial
hybridity, and the yearning that is laden with hatred is epitomized when
Steward shoots "the white girl first," a girl whose "whiteness" is surely
facetiously imposed on her by a town who would have expelled her if
she was truly "white" (1).[12] Deacon and K.D.'s privileging of racial purity
while yearning racially (and sexually) for impure female bodies creates a
self-loathing that both men project onto the women. Gigi and Consolata
stand in stark opposition to the women of Ruby who "did not powder
their faces and they wore no harlot's perfume"—women who are not slack
or slovenly, neglecting to begin canning in a timely manner (5, 143). Deacon and K.D.'s desire for difference, in this case racial impurity, is at odds
with Ruby's unwritten law of racial purity. Deacon in particular is tor-
mented by the horror he is instructed to feel toward miscegenation and
the pervasive desire for racial mixture that permeates his mind and body.

Consolata's transgressive acts are not the only root of Deacon's fear.
His fear is also based in his own uncontrollable desire for racial impurity.
In "Consumerism, or the Cultural Logic of Late Cannibalism," Crystal
Bartolovich draws on Peter Stallybrass's and Allon White's assertion in
their study on transgression when she explains the paradox of desire and
impurity, "The low," that is, dirty, contaminated "was internalized under
the sign of negation and disgust. . . . But disgust always bears the imprint
of desire" (223). The truth of disgust bearing the imprint of desire is epitomized by Deacon's impression and remembrance of nineteen Negro ladies
in an unnamed prosperous colored town. Beginning in 1910, Big Daddy,
Deacon's and Steward's father, and his brother Pryor began traveling to
other colored towns to "examine, review and judge" them. During one
of the later trips, Deacon recalls that he and Steward watched nineteen

creamy-skinned, well-dressed, immaculately coiffed Negro ladies pose for a photograph. As the women passed Deacon and Steward, the twins simultaneously fell off the railing they were sitting on and proceeded to wrestle, which garnered them the smiles they desired. As an adult, Deacon reminisces, "Even now the verbena scent was clear; even now the summer dresses, the creamy, sunlit skin excited him" (110).

These vivacious women embody the separation the founding fathers encountered when they embarked on their journey, walking from Mississippi and Louisiana to Oklahoma. These hopeful men and women who thought they were escaping the division between free and slave and rich and poor were inconsolably disappointed to find ". . . a new separation: light-skinned against black," and thus, "The sign of racial purity they had taken for granted had become a stain" (194). Deacon's enrapture and desire for the nineteen ladies with creamy and luminous skin goes against everything that Ruby stands for and believes in. Deacon's inability to reconcile his own Du Boisian "warring ideals" is evident in his fascination with the nineteen creamy-skinned women and later with his initial captivation with Consolata and her "amazing" mint-leaf-green eyes.

Although Deacon's contempt for Consolata would suggest that it was she who seduced him, the opposite is true. He is the one who arrives at her *garden,* inviting her to enter a forbidden courtship. In this sense, Deacon is the quintessential snake in the garden. Deacon's interest in Consolata began at the same derby race at which she determined she already knew the people of Ruby. The moment was marked by an unspoken mutual eroticism:

It was while Consolata waited on the steps that she saw him for the first time. Sha sha sha. Sha sha sha. A lean young man astride one horse, leading another. . . . His hips were rocking in the saddle, back and forth, back and forth. Sha sha sha. Sha sha sha. Consolata saw his profile, and the wing of a feathered thing, undead, fluttered in her stomach. . . . Just as she opened the passenger door he passed again. On foot, running lightly, eager to return to the festive knot of people farther down the road. Casually, perfunctorily, he looked her way. Consolata looked back and thought she saw hesitation in his eyes if not in his stride. Quickly she ducked into the sun-baked Mercury, where the heat seemed to explain her difficult

breathing. She did not see him again for two months of time made un-
stable by a feathered thing fighting for wingspread. . . . So she did the yard
chores at first light and spent the balance of the day inside, mismanag-
ing her work. None of which helped in the end. *He came to her.* (226–28,
emphasis mine)

The language in this passage, as well as in a later description of Consolata's cellar preparation for a Candomblé ritual draws on Haitian Vodou, too, and offers a compelling complementary reading to the incestuous analysis above, helping to reveal how the Convent women become at
home in diaspora.

READING VODOU IN *PARADISE*

The "Sha sha sha. Sha sha sha" that permeates Consolata's and Deacon's
relationship and represents Consolata's desire for Deacon has multiple
significations. The first "Sha sha sha. Sha sha sha" is in direct correlation
with Deacon's sensual horseback riding, suggesting that the "shas" have a
connection to horses as well. "Sha sha sha. Sha sha sha" sounds like the
soft, guided movement of a horse being ridden and the brushing movement of the horse's mane and tail.[13] Consolata's association of Deacon
with a sha-sound also resonates with Vodou spirit mounting—the *lwa*,
Vodou god, mounts the *cheval*, human. Consolata's history and characteristics both parallel the Vodou Goddess of Love, Ezili, and are at odds with
her.[14] Joan Dayan explains that Ezili is a goddess who is unique to Haiti—
a "New World" goddess who has no precedent in Yoruba or Dahomey.
Dayan contrasts spirit possession and slave-master possession when explaining Ezili's relationship to the function of memory. She explains that
the spirit mounting of the human is a form of possession, and Ezili comes
to represent "something like collective physical remembrance" that gives
"substance" to "an experience of domination" (56). The experience of
domination that Dayan refers to is specific to the slave master possessing
the slave woman's body.

Ezili is a phenomenon of the Americas' "contact zone," a phenomenon
born out of cultural syncretism. Unlike Damballa or Ogoun, she had no
pre-existence as a Yoruba or Dahomey deity; rather she was born on Hai-

tian soil in response to "New World" needs. Her birth is catalyzed by a slave system in which black women's bodies are denied sanctity. As a result, according to Dayan, when Ezili enters a woman or man, "together they re-create and reinterpret a history of mastery and servitude" (60). Like Ezili, Consolata wants to repair the damages produced in the contact zone. She wants to be homed through her relationship with Deacon. She desires the new form of knowledge that is created when Ezili enters a man or woman and re-creates and reinterprets history and by doing so creates a space for someone like Consolata, who *is* in fact transnational by virtue of her Brazilian birth, to actually embrace a transnational identity. In other words, although Consolata is already transnational as it is popularly and literally understood, the way that Catholicism has stifled her ability to achieve the "more" Lone insists folk sometimes need has limited her ability to possess a transnational identity. As a rite of passage prior to her confirmation, Mary Magna impressed upon Consolata that "God's generosity . . . is nowhere better seen than in the gift of patience." This lesson prevents Consolata from noticing the things that she is losing, the first being her first language (*Paradise* 242). Language is a significant link to community and belonging, so although Portuguese is not spoken in Ruby, encountering the residents of Ruby nonetheless triggers lost memories of community, kinship, and culture that make Consolata realize all too well that she does not feel at home in diaspora. The home and community that Consolata desires, however, is at odds with every body of knowledge that shapes Deacon's understanding and location of home.

In a reverse of how Ezili demands luxurious offerings from her devotees, Consolata offers Deacon luxuries when she invites him to her house and offers him pears, fancy wines, pillow slips crammed with rosemary, and linen sheets rinsed in hot water steeped in cinnamon in a cellar room that sparkles "in the light of an eight-holder candelabra from Holland and reeked of ancient herbs" (237). What was intended to entice Deacon in fact repulses him, and he insists that ". . . a beautiful, golden-skinned, outside woman with moss-green eyes that tried to trap a man, close him up in a cellar room with liquor to enfeeble him so they could do carnal things, unnatural things in the dark" (279). It is not the implied romance that Consolata is offering Deacon that makes him buck; instead it is the absolute danger that is involved in the consummation of the transnational home that she imagines she can create through Deacon.

Although I am not arguing that Consolata embodies fully Ezili's attributes, it is productive to consider the attributes that they do share. Ezili is often described as the pale goddess of love, as virginal, and as prostituted. Consolata is subjected to "dirty pokings" during her ninth year; yet, after thirty celibate years she has a sort of virginal essence when she commences the affair with Deacon. Dayan draws upon Ezili's contradictory identities when she discusses "love" and mulatto mistresses. She argues that as the lwa of love "Ezili demands that the word be reinvented" (63). Dayan explains how a Victorian "cult of true womanhood"[15] positioned white women as pure, chaste, and virtuous, while black women were positioned as lustful and impure, creating the space for white men to violate black women without accountability. She notes how mulatta women's in-betweenness "somehow became the concrete signifier for lust that could be portrayed as 'love' . . . [i]f, in the perverse ethics of the planter, the spiritualized, refined images of white women depended on the violation of black women, the bleached-out sable Venus accommodated both extremes" (56–57). The mulatta mistress thus became the ideal; white men viewed them as sexual, yet pure and beautiful. Their duality as prostitute and lover often placed mulatta women in paradoxical and vulnerable positions—cared for and adored while simultaneously "excluded from marriage, threatened by poverty, and often abandoned" (57). As the pale, virginal, goddess of love, Ezili interrogates what "love" means in diasporic life. Dayan's perception of Ezili as interrogator and Consolata's mimicry of her attributes provide a space to examine intersections between "love" and cultural and religious syncretism in *Paradise*.

TOWARD A SELF-LOVE ETHIC

I do not intend to give an in-depth review of critical discourse on "love" in diasporic and postcolonial cultures, but I do want to make note of the emergence of the idea of "love" in a variety of critical discourses. Chela Sandoval employs Roland Barthes's *A Lover's Discourse* in *Methodology of the Oppressed: Theory Out of Bounds* to argue that romantic love, combined with risk and courage, creates the possibility for social change. In *Race*

Matters, Cornel West argues that black people must replace nihilism with a "love ethic" that privileges "self-love and love of others," which he proposes would increase "self-valuation" and encourage "political resistance in one's community" (29–30). bell hooks has an entire series on "black love." hooks argues the nation is moving away from love and love is the only hope for achieving an earthly paradise in *All About Love: New Visions.* Morrison seems to also have an investment in interrogating the idea of love. Her eighth novel is titled *Love.* The idea of loving one's children to death consumes *Beloved,* which is about the "freedom" to love. These disparate discourses on love are not so different. Each is entrenched in concepts of self-love, respect, and forgiveness. *Paradise* falls squarely in the center of these concepts.

After a heated debate with Pat Best over the relevance of Africa to Ruby, Richard Misner concedes that Ruby loves their children to death (*Paradise* 210). Consolata's analysis of the Convent women is that they are full of "foolish babygirl wishes," which do not bother her nearly as much as their hopes for love: "One by one they would float down the stairs . . . to sit on the floor and talk of love as if they knew anything at all about it. They spoke of men who came to caress them in their sleep; of men waiting for them in the desert or by cool water; of men who once had desperately loved them; or men who should have loved them, might have loved, would have" (222).

Penny and Clarissa, the Arapaho Indian girls detained at the Convent, view Consolata's behavior as she prepares the cellar and eventually accepts that Deacon is not coming as "serious instruction about the limits and possibilities of love and imprisonment . . ." (238). In reference to Christ's crucifixion, Richard Misner, the outsider minister of Calvary Baptist Church, contends, "This execution made it possible to respect— freely, not in fear—one's self and one another. Which was what love was: *unmotivated respect*" (146 emphasis mine). These disparate references to love converge during Senior Pulliam's and Richard Misner's matrimonial sermons at K.D.'s and Arnette's wedding. Pulliam, the local Methodist minister, directs his sermon at Richard Misner and asserts, "Love is divine only and difficult always. If you think it is easy you are a fool. If you think it is natural you are blind. It is a learned application without reason or motive except that it is God" (141). In response, Misner unhooks the cross that hung on the rear wall of the church and stands unspeaking before the congregation, hoping that his silent demonstration will convey the necessity of "unmotivated respect" for any relationship to thrive.

Out of all this discourse on love emerges a truth: Ruby loved itself too much, and the Convent women did not love themselves enough. Visitors offer a way to synthesize these disparities; they function as an act of grace that offers Ruby and the Convent women the opportunity to reconcile their pasts so that they might learn the liberating value of the "unmotivated respect" Misner calls for and learn to practice the self-love they all so desperately need. Visitors are the link between love and critical appropriations in *Paradise* because they reflect the possibility of being at home in diaspora, of knowing one's self in a way that is not framed by nation or identity politics, but that reflects a complex and diverse body of knowledge.

Visitors may or may not be real, but they are real to those who are visited. The primary purpose of visitors is their potential to assist the visited in navigating the path of "self-love," and visitors offer the visited alternative ways of knowing. The kind of alternative knowledge that visitors offer varies depending on the character being visited, but in all cases the knowledge challenges familiar, comfortable epistemologies. The challenge that the alternative ways of knowing offer the visited is an act of grace—an offer that if accepted promises the receiver new insight that enables her to love herself in spite of past faults or what others might think. Visitors, then, are liminal figures that stand in the threshold between the real and unreal. I use *liminal* here in the anthropological sense of the term, particularly in the way it is applied in the work of British cultural anthropologist Victor Turner, who lived with the Ndembu of Zambia for five years studying ritual society. According to Turner, *liminality* is a space where human beings are temporarily caught within a social structure, a space where they can become most aware of themselves.[16] The space that visitors invite the visited to enter into has the potential of elevating self-consciousness, and the knowledge gained in that space is a kind of ritualistic rite of passage that is liberating. Only Consolata crosses the threshold, however, and completes the initiation process. Both Soane and Dovey remain so deeply steeped in Western ways of knowing they are unable to accept the visitor's offer to guide them through the midpoint in the rite.

The first notion of a visitor is in the chapter titled "Seneca," and the visitor is simply referred to as "Dovey's friend." This chapter opens with a vague reference to scratching on windowpanes and someone who never comes at night. Later, Dovey concludes that, since she cannot determine which side of the Oven debate is correct, the teenagers or the grown folk, she will bring the matter to "her friend" on his next visit.[17] Dovey's friend does not appear at the ranch outside of town that Steward is so proud of; instead he appears at a little foreclosure home on St. Matthews Street that Steward and Deacon never sold. It is this house, the house that "was close to her sister, to Mount Calvary, the Women's Club," and most importantly the place "where her Friend chose to pay his calls," that becomes "more and more home to Dovey" (88).

There is "a sign" the first time Dovey's friend appears. "Butterflies. A trembling highway of persimmon-colored wings cut across the green tree-tops forever—then vanished" (90–91). Later that same day, sitting under the trees decorated previously by butterfly wings, Dovey meets her friend for the first time as he is cutting through her yard. Although she cannot identify him as a local Ruby resident, she begins speaking to him almost incessantly about the butterflies and the house on St. Matthews Street.[18] After that initial visit, Dovey's friend returns every month or two, and Dovey finds more and more reasons to stay at the house on St. Matthews Street. Despite her joy in seeing her Friend, Dovey cannot help but think she talks nonsense when he comes: "Things she didn't know were on her mind. Pleasures, worries, things unrelated to the world's serious issues. Yet he listened intently to whatever she said," and although he "seemed hers alone . . . by a divining she could not explain, she knew that once she asked him his name, he would never come again" (92).

Both the butterflies and the incessant chatter that her friend conjures symbolize the stifling nature of life in Ruby, especially for the lives of women. Ruby has defined itself with nationalistic and puritanical rhetoric that polices the behavior of women. The disgust that the murderous men of Ruby feel toward the Convent women when they decide to slaughter them is driven by their perception of these women not fitting the tenets of the "cult of true womanhood" that they have imposed upon women in Ruby. As a consequence, Dovey, like all women in Ruby, is silenced until her friend arrives accompanied by butterflies, symbols of the metaphorical new birth Dovey could experience if she allows her mind to be opened to forms of knowledge that extend beyond and often threaten the ways of knowing and being that define Ruby.

After K.D., Dovey's nephew by marriage, and Arnette are finally married and take over the foreclosed house, Dovey's friend only comes to her once more ". . . in a dream where he was moving away from her. She called; he turned. Next thing she knew, she was washing his hair," and she awakes with shampoo suds on her hands (287). The disappearance of Dovey's visitor coinciding with the arrival of the purported next patriarch of Ruby is not surprising. K.D.'s ego is wounded terribly when Gigi uses him as a boy-toy and discards him when she becomes bored with him. Arnette is given refuge at the Convent when she is pregnant with K.D.'s out-of-wedlock child and uses a broomstick handle to abort the pregnancy. Neither K.D. nor Arnette appreciated that the Convent was ultimately a space where "unmotivated respect" was extended freely. Their presence in the house on St. Matthews Street precludes the possibility of crossing a threshold that is metaphysical and framed by the desire to leave behind old ways of knowing.

Soane's visit is singular in occurrence, and she is also visited in the "Seneca" chapter. Both sisters being visited is significant because the chapter focuses heavily on loss. It opens with Dovey reflecting on Steward's loss of taste and Dovey recounting the many losses Steward experienced between their marriage in 1949 and 1973, the year during which the chapter is set. "Almost always, these nights, when Dovey Morgan thought about her husband it was in terms of what he had lost. . . . Contrary to his (and all of Ruby's) assessment, the more Steward acquired, the more visible his losses." He was defeated in a statewide election for church secretary; he lost land and trees in order to allow natural gas to be drilled at his ranch; he lost his hairline; and "in 1964, when he was forty, Fairy's curse came true: they learned neither could ever have children" (82). Steward's losses are highlighted by not simply the debate between the teenagers and the adults over the words on the Oven, but also the utility of the Oven. Post–World War II economic prosperity and technological advancements provided the women of Ruby with both time and no need for a wood-burning oven (89). Thus, in spite of understanding the behavior of the youth to be rebellious and disrespectful, the women of Ruby resented the Oven. "Minus the baptisms the Oven had no real value," Soane reflects, "What was needed back in Haven's early days had never been needed in Ruby. . . . A utility became a shrine" (103). The loss of the utility of the Oven accompanied by the many losses of Steward and particularly the loss of a Morgan family line—Dovey and Steward cannot have children, Soane and Deacon lost their two sons in the Vietnam War, and the other Morgan brother's (Elder's) children had all left Ruby—sheds light on Soane's brief but meaningful visit.

While Soane is hanging laundry and thinking about the abortion Consolata helped her with nineteen years earlier, she spots "a lady in her yard smiling. She wore a brown wool gown and a white linen old-timey bonnet and carried a peck basket" (102). Unlike Dovey's friend, Soane recognizes the woman as a "stranger." After waving to Soane, the woman turns and walks away, causing Soane to notice two things: "the basket was empty but the lady carried it with two hands as though it were full, which, as she knew now, was a sign of what was to come—an emptiness that would weigh her down, and absence too heavy to carry. And she knew who sent the lady to tell her so" (102). While "who" sent the lady could be left open for speculation, what the woman and her visit represent is clear. The massacre at the Convent occurs three years later, in 1976, and Soane openly expresses her grief and disappointment about the event when she arrives at the Convent with Dovey in the immediate aftermath of the murders.

> The sisters cover Consolata with the sheet.
> "I didn't know her as well as you," Dovey says.
> "I loved her. As God is my witness I did, but nobody knew her really."
> "Why did they do it?"
> "They? You mean 'he,' don't you? Steward killed her. Not Deek."
> "You make it sound as though it's all his fault."
> "I didn't mean to."
> "Then what? What did you mean?"
> Soane does not know what she means, other than how to locate a sliver of soap to clean away any little taint she can. But it is an exchange that alters their relationship irrevocably. (291–92)

In contrast to her sister, Soane is more perceptive about the purpose of her visit, which perhaps is why she is only visited once. Soane makes no public declarations against Ruby and its narrow ways, but she does have her own thoughts, and she holds opinions that are not always aligned with her husband, the voice and mind of Ruby. Her desire and willingness to think for herself result in an enduring friendship with Consolata in spite of the affair Consolata had with Soane's husband, Deacon (Consolata "steps in" to save the life of Soane's son after a car accident). Soane insists that the women at the Convent are not evil, just "different," when she is driving to the Convent with Dovey after being warned by Lone that their husbands are part of the mob that is headed out there (288). And years earlier, she insists that anyone who was offered refuge at the Convent "must be all right" when Deek berates Gigi and accuses Soane of being "partial to those women out there" (105). The self-assuredness that is reflected in the friendly yet serious banter that Soane engages in with Deek causes mild consternation for him: "Deek reassured himself with more force than confidence, for he was increasingly uneasy about Soane. Nothing he could put his fingernail under, just a steady sense of losing ground" (112). The uneasiness Deek feels about Soane is produced by her elevated self-consciousness and knowledge that allows her to think for herself. Soane, however, exhibits no clear intentions of pursuing any actions that would indeed move her through the threshold so that she might experience grace, particularly for the loss of her sons and the "sin" she committed when she lost her unborn child.

Chronologically, Consolata is visited last. Like Soane, she, too, is able to understand the purpose of her visitor, but in contrast to Soane, Consolata goes beyond registering that there are alternative ways of knowing than those she is familiar with and actually responds to her visit with immediate action. Consolata's visitor offers her an alternative from the Catholicism of Mary Magna, and he challenges Consolata to dredge up memories from "far country," the place he insists she knows him from. Feeling the disappointment of unrequited love (Deacon's) and the fear of dying alone, Consolata abandons God: "'I'll miss You,' she told Him. 'I really will (251)'"; her visitor appears immediately after. He looks like a younger, male version of her: long, tea-colored hair and apple-green eyes. In a flirtatious and seductive manner, he insists, "Come on, girl.

You know me," and that he is from "far country" (252). His presence produces a comfort and lightness in Consolata that contrasts sharply with the
depressant, apathetic mood she was in when she said farewell to Mary
Magna's god and ultimately gave up on life. Upon the departure of her
visitor, Consolata transforms from Connie, the drunken, death-seeking
woman in the cellar, to Consolata Sosa, the reverent, wizened woman
who leads the Convent women through Candomblé-based rituals of self-
reinvention and reconciliation.[19] While the nationalistic conception of
home that Deacon embraces fails to "home" Consolata, her visitor expels
her feelings of homelessness when he proposes that the losses she mourns
can be regained not through the primordial past, but through a present
that embraces syncretic epistemologies of home that rely on a mélange of
diasporic theories of identity.

Passing through the threshold is ultimately an act of being born again.
The self-love that is produced by the alternative knowledge on the other
side of the threshold functions as an act of grace that enables Consolata
to identify a way to negotiate living. Her visitor and the knowledge that
he offers provide the "something more" that Lone tells Consolata folk
sometimes need. When Consolata, who embodies qualities that signify
on the Vodou priestess Ezili, *re-members*—as Morrison's character Sethe
in *Beloved* describes acts of remembering again—Candomblé rituals, Consolata embraces forgotten diasporic theories of cultural identity when
she leads the Convent women through the healing rituals. Her guidance
and instruction offer African American women a space at the center of
transnationalism—a space that does not require crossing international
boundaries, and a space that would compel à careful observer to realize,
". . . unlike some people in Ruby, the Convent women were no longer
haunted" (266).

NEGOTIATING THE TRANSNATIONAL

Consolata's visitor invites her to pass through an epistemological threshold. The alternative knowledge on the other side of the threshold is represented through the Candomblé-like rituals the Convent women practice, but it is also represented through the epigraph at the opening of the
novel and the character, Piedade, who is referenced several times after

Consolata is visited. Both Piedade and Consolata's visitor play a critical role in enabling the Convent women to negotiate transnational identities. Consolata introduces the Convent women to Piedade through narrative during the initiation process. In Portuguese, Piedade means "pity," and it can be inferred that Consolata understands her to be "the god who sought her out in the garden" via Consolata's visitor (283). Piedade is not a god or priestess in any European, African, or American religions. Yet the way Consolata describes her to the Convent women positions Piedade at the head of a diasporic pantheon of gods, orishas, lwas, and saints charged with intervening in Ruby's and the Convent women's lives, reminding them, "Perhaps the achievement of Paradise was premature, a little hasty if no one could take the time to understand other languages, other views, other narratives period" (Morrison, "Nobel"). When Consolata describes Piedade and presumably the place where Piedade dwells, she describes beauty, riches, songs, food, and general tranquility—a kind of non-denominational, heterogeneous home space where "gods and goddesses sat in the pews with the congregation" (*Paradise*, 263–64, 285).

Piedade's consistent affiliation with the sea and water, particularly in the last page of the narrative, situate her as a goddess of love and grace for subaltern people. The final page of the narrative describes a singing woman "black as firewood" seated next to a younger woman whose head rests on her lap. The black woman whose face is framed in cerulean blue trolls her ruined fingers through the younger woman's tea-brown hair, while the younger woman's emerald eyes adore the black face. They are surrounded by beach full of sea trash, discarded bottle caps, a broken sandal, and a small dead radio playing the quite surf. The black woman in cerulean blue is Piedade, Consolata's muse, who simultaneously resembles the Yoruba priestess, Yemanjá, and the Virgin Mary.[20] The woman with tea-colored hair and emerald eyes is the born-again Consolata. During the massacre, Connie, dressed in blue and white, "stepped-in" and revived the "white girl," but Connie herself does not resurrect; instead she lives in this space with Piedade, "down here in Paradise" (318).

When reading the final page of the text, Piedade's song sung on a beach amidst sea trash does not sound utopian, particularly since her constant song throughout the text is reminiscent of W. E. B. Du Bois's "Sorrow Songs," which he tells us ". . . are the music of an unhappy people, of the children of disappointment; they tell of death and suffering and unvoiced longing toward a truer world, of misty wanderings and hidden ways." Yet, perhaps like the slaves' Sorrow Songs, Piedade's songs are full of hope: "Through all the sorrow of the Sorrow Songs there breathes a hope—a faith in the ultimate justice of things . . . sometime, somewhere, men will judge men by their souls and not by their skins" (Du Bois 188). The paradoxical nature of both the space Piedade occupies and the function of the Sorrow Songs resonates with Richard Misner's eulogy for Save-Marie at the conclusion of the narrative when he encourages the attendees to not think about "death being the only democracy" but to instead think about why the child has died (295). The idea that death is the only democracy implies that African Americans can only experience social and political equality in the United States in the afterlife. Considering why death occurs and how one might avoid death is a productive task for Ruby in the post-massacre moment.

The contradiction in Piedade's songs is also present in the epigraph of the novel. The epigraph from "The Thunder: Perfect Mind," a Gnostic text, opens *Paradise* with ideas that challenge most people's understanding of redemption.[21] The epigraph reads:

> For many are the pleasant forms which exist in
> numerous sins,
> and incontinencies,
> and disgraceful passions
> and fleeting pleasures,
> which (men) embrace until they become
> sober
> and go up to their resting place.
> And they will find me there,
> and they will live,
> and they will not die again.[22]

There are two main ways in which this passage challenges typical Western belief systems. It contradicts the Judeo-Christian notion that sins and disgraceful passions will bar the unrepentant soul from heaven by suggesting that men who embrace sins, incontinences, passions, and pleasures are admitted into the Holy Kingdom. The second challenge, which is really more of a radical disruption, is that the speaker of this text is female. Just as the suggestions in the text contradict Judeo-Christian doctrine, the female speaker's description of herself is a contradiction as well:

> I am the whore and the holy one.
> I am the wife and the virgin.
> I am the mother and the daughter [. . .]
> I am the barren one and many are her sons [. . .]
> I am the bride and the bridegroom [. . .]
> I am the one whom they call Life, and you have called Death.
> I am the one whom they call Law, and you have called Lawlessness.
>   ("The Thunder")

These paradoxes resemble those of the "new world" goddess of love, Ezili, who offers a striking parallel to Consolata. The narrator's promises and self-description in "Thunder" sound familiar as well. As Consolata's orisha, Piedade, the woman who "sang but never says a word," makes similar promises of re-birth and eternal life for Consolata and the Convent women, women who are broken, abused, and used. Piedade, like the divinity in "Thunder," also does not represent the traditional and perfected divine. The combination of the paradoxes and the conception of salvation that is antithetical to Judeo-Christian doctrine resonate with the syncretic blending of Christianity, Candomblé, Vodou, Catholicism, and Gnosticism to achieve the "more" that folk sometimes need.

The paradoxes in "Thunder" push the hearers to unravel the divinity's mysteries and understand how a harlot can indeed be holy and how a barren woman can have many children. There are those who simply hear the words of the divine, and then there are those who receive the words with a divine knowledge—a knowledge that is heterogeneous by nature and invested in alternative ways of knowing. This alternative is well received by Consolata and the Convent women but is scorned by Ruby. Ruby has a twisted and ultimately deadly notion of self-love. The Convent women, however, come to know themselves through a syncretic blending of diasporic theories of cultural identity. Paradise is a not an immortal space, as the 8-rocks would like to think; Paradise is a messy space that must be flexible and embrace fluidity or risk chaos.

Indeed, Ruby itself might also experience the grace that the Convent women achieved. Doubting the truth of a "mass disappearance" at the Convent, Anna Flood and Richard Misner go to the Convent and inspect the site. During their investigation, Anna decides to fight the chickens for five umber-colored eggs that she thought were fresh, which Richard wraps with a white handkerchief. After retrieving these eggs from the henhouse, Richard and Anna see what one describes as a window and the other describes as a door: "It was when they returned . . . that they saw it. Or sensed it, rather, for there was nothing to see. A door, she said later. 'No, a window,' he said. . . . They expanded on the subject: What did a door mean? what a window? focusing on the sign rather than the event; excited by the invitation rather than the party. They knew it was there. Knew it so well they were transfixed for a long moment before they backed away and ran to the car." Speculating about "[w]ho saw a closed door; who saw a raised window. Anything to avoid reliving the shiver or saying out loud what they were wondering. Whether through a door needing to be opened or a beckoning window already raised, what would happen if you entered? What would be on the other side? What on earth would it be?" (305).

The retrieval of the eggs and the vision of a door/window are pivotal occurrences that address the potential for Ruby to rethink home. Through critical appropriations of diasporic theories of cultural identity, the Convent women develop a sense of home and community that allows them to know themselves and to love themselves. The sense of home they develop is neither a nationalist location nor a primordial location but instead a frequently reoccurring trope in African American women's writing. Home is contingent upon embracing unfamiliar, yet homely spaces that in the case of the Convent women are spaces in which they can embrace a transnational identity. The closed door/raised window, then, is indicative of an alternative way to live in a *racial house*. In her essay "Home," Toni Morrison ponders "how to convert a racist house into a race-specific yet nonracist home" (5). She explains that, if she must ". . . live in a racial house, it was important [. . .] to rebuild it so that it was not a windowless prison into which [. . .] no cry could be heard, but rather an open house, grounded, yet generous in its supply of windows and doors" (4). The creation of the door/window in the henhouse creates the possibility for Anna and Richard to remain hopeful and perhaps lead Ruby toward a different way of understanding home and nation, an understanding that extends beyond national boundaries, without ever leaving home. Such an understanding would lay a foundation for the unmotivated respect that Ruby lacks in its relationship with the Convent women.

Whether Anna and Richard saw a closed door or a raised window is not significant; the invitation and inquisition about what is on the other side are central to understanding the alternative that this unknown space offers. The Convent women find the "something more" that Lone insists folk sometimes need when they embrace alternative ways of knowing. Now, Anna and Richard, not 8-rocks, but extensions of Ruby nonetheless, are also offered an alternative. The open ending of the novel requires that the reader can only speculate on Richard's and Anna's decision; however, the fact that immediately after Richard's eulogist claim that "what is sown is not alive until it dies," he sees the window in the garden once again and "felt it beckon toward another place—neither life nor death—but there, just yonder, shaping thoughts he did not know he had," allows for hopeful speculation (307). He hopes that Ruby, like the Convent women, can indeed embrace alternatives and experience grace—an experience that will free them from the constant reminder of being disallowed and unequal in a nation that touts democratic ideals of equality and justice for all.

What *Paradise* exhibits most profoundly is that, more than thirty years after the civil rights movement and over twenty years after the rise of black feminist criticism, all the women are still white and all the blacks are still men.[23] For Morrison, bravery is not just vocal, but it is also the black woman who is prepared to recover her losses by any means necessary. The Convent women return packing guns, brandishing swords, and decked out in military fatigues. Unaware of their return, Billie Delia questions: "When will they return? When will they reappear, with blazing eyes, war paint and huge hands to rip up and stomp down this prison calling itself a town? . . . A backward noplace ruled by men whose power to control was out of control and who had the nerve to say who could live and who not and where; who had seen in lively, free, unarmed females the mutiny of the mares and so got rid of them" (308).

Despite the Convent women's apparent preparedness for war, interpreting their return as one bound up in acts of revenge is not as productive as an interpretation that understands that the space "just yonder" where unmotivated respect reigns is not yet fully accessible. The inaccessibility of a space that embodies a critical gender consciousness presents notable challenges not only for the black woman artist in the United States who is trying to negotiate transnational politics, but the inaccessibility also has ramifications for post-national discourse in African American studies. Ruby's rigidity and the massacre of the Convent women emphatically register the challenge of home being paradise.

While the Convent women do indeed experience an act of grace when their critical appropriations enable them to embrace transnational identities that make them feel at home, the fact that they only experience grace through death—metaphorical or physical—raises serious concerns. Billie Delia's questions suggest that being armed is necessary for women "down here in Paradise." The paradisiacal space that Richard Misner likes to believe is "just yonder" is inaccessible in *Paradise* due to patriarchal-informed ideologies of nationalism that push African American women to the margins of communities and society. The ultimate challenge in *Paradise*, then, is not embracing a transnational identity, but the impossibility of belonging in any community.

CHAPTER 2

Romanticizing Diaspora and Remembering Zora in Erna Brodber's *Louisiana*

The concept of diaspora can produce romantic conceptions of community and kinship that are steeped in homogeneity. Conceptualizing diaspora as a fixed and homogenous state of being is rooted in essentialist ideas of origin and authenticity that fail to register identity as the "production" that Stuart Hall insists is never complete and always in process. Erna Brodber's *Louisiana* is filled with characters that are displaced either domestically or internationally from places they identify as home, or they simply are unable to identify a particular place as home. Pan-Africanism, négritude and Vodou are appropriated in *Louisiana* in order to assist diasporic subjects in negotiating the presence of one nation—a marginalized black nation—within another—the dominant white nation. While I will attend to these diasporic theories, I am more interested in how anthropology is positioned in the narrative as a site of empowerment for people of African descent, a group that has had a vexed relationship with anthropology. In *Louisiana* a palimpsest narrative emerges in which the life and experiences of the protagonist, Ella Townsend Kohl, signifies on and memorializes the life and work of Floridian anthropologist, folklorist, and writer Zora Neale Hurston. A close examination of this palimpsest narrative identifies trans-historical challenges with community and gender that black women have faced when attempting to locate physical and intellectual home spaces.

Analysis of the palimpsest narrative that Brodber creates when Ella's life and experiences are written over those of Zora Neal Hurston is critical for understanding how blackness and femaleness create challenges for African American women who possess transnational sensibilities. While doing anthropological fieldwork in Louisiana, Ella learns to question Western constructions of history and productions of knowledge, much as Hurston insisted on recording and revering folk culture when such work was far from common. The new form of knowledge that Ella acquires once she reclaims the field of anthropology is complicated by gender, particularly by the intersection of what Sigmund Freud referred to as "work and love." Ella, like her real-life parallel, Hurston, has to make a choice between work and pleasure, whether sexual or social. *Louisiana* offers the opportunity to examine whether the gender constraints placed on Hurston's work and life during the pre–civil rights era are imagined differently when her work and life are reconstructed during the post–civil rights era. Despite the advances gained by social movements in the 1970s, gender constraints in *Louisiana* exemplify how race and gender converge and make developing a transnational identity a vexed endeavor. In spite of the "cures" that Brodber offers through claiming the field of anthropology and appropriating theories of Pan-Africanism, négritude, and Vodou, the protagonist she creates in the post–civil rights era is just as limited in voice and the ability to enjoy both work and pleasure as were Hurston herself and Hurston's protagonist, Janie Crawford, in *Their Eyes Were Watching God*. Ella's barrenness and her eventual unexplainable and premature death can be read as a palimpsest of Hurston's life and work and are exemplary of the challenges that African American women face when being excluded from transnational discourse.[1]

Like *Paradise, Louisiana* leaves many readers confused. Because both the style and language that Brodber uses can make understanding basic elements of the narrative challenging, I want to first provide a synopsis of the narrative. I will then explain how anthropology affects the process of becoming that Ella goes through before moving to an analysis of Ella and Hurston.

Ella Townsend is a Columbia University graduate student in the Department of Anthropology. Her parents are Jamaican immigrants who not only give up their Jamaican cultural identity to pursue the "American Dream," but who also fail to develop any significant relationship with Ella, their only child. As an anthropology graduate student, Ella is commissioned by Franklin D. Roosevelt's Works Progress Administration (WPA) to record the history of the blacks of southwest Louisiana. Ella arrives in Franklin, Louisiana, with predetermined notions of science, knowledge, and truth that are challenged by the local culture. Shortly after her arrival, her soon-to-be husband and fellow anthropologist, Reuben Kohl, joins Ella. Like Ella, Reuben is trained in anthropology, but he abandons his academic career for one in music. Also like Ella, Reuben is a migratory subject of the African diaspora with his roots in the Congo and Europe. Together, Ella and Reuben work to establish a sense of home in Franklin, and later in New Orleans.

Ella's fieldwork is unexpectedly complicated when her informant, Sue Ann Grant-King, a.k.a. Mammy, dies before completing their interview sessions. Sue Ann's death becomes of little consequence, however, when Sue Ann and her long-dead Jamaican friend, Lowly, begin speaking to Ella from the dead. Sue Ann and Lowly speak to Ella through the recording machine the Department of Anthropology provided for Ella to collect the interviews. The recording machine functions as a metaphor for the untold story of the interconnectedness of the African diaspora that is evidenced through the machine's uncanny ability to record what has not been said. Only at the novel's end does Ella, with the aid of Reuben and the deceased "venerable sisters" (*Louisiana* 32), as she comes to call Sue Ann and Lowly, piece together Sue Ann and Lowly's stories. In doing so, she learns that Sue Ann was a psychic and a Garvey UNIA organizer, and that Lowly, Sue Ann, and Silas, Sue Ann's husband, all worked tirelessly to resist hegemony and proselytize Pan-Africanist ideologies, uniting black people in the United States regardless of national origins.

ANTHROPOLOGY AND THE LITERARY NARRATIVE

When Ella arrives in Franklin, Louisiana, she has neither thought critically about Western notions of science and ways of being nor considered the irony of a black woman studying anthropology. The original philosophy of anthropology is one that is indebted to the pseudo-science of the European Enlightenment that fueled the racist ideologies that would justify the transatlantic slave trade as well as Nazi eugenics. During the Enlightenment, or "age of reason," a vast number of European philosophers, geographers, and physicians wrote treatises that ordered everything from flora and fauna to humankind. In the ordering of humankind, people of African descent were placed at the bottom of the hierarchy and described as uncivilized, barbaric, and incapable of independent thought. During this period, the "idea" of race emerges as Europe moves from a system of difference that distinguishes people based upon religion to a system rooted in physical difference. Social anthropologist Faye V. Harrison explains how, in its early formation as a discipline, anthropology was concerned with "the elaboration of typologies and techniques for classifying and operationalizing the discrete 'races of man.'" Thus, "The key constructs of culture and evolution, which set the terms for early anthropological inquiry, often were invested with essentialist and universalized 'biomoral' assumptions concerning the natural history of human variation" ("Persistent Power" 50). It is not until World War II and the genocide that ensued under Hitler's Nazi regime that significant antiracist work began to emerge in the study of anthropology.

While there were some African American physical anthropologists who produced antiracist research in the years prior to World War II,[2] the German American anthropologist Franz Boas is most noted for introducing a liberalism that "limited race's meaning to biophysical and morphological characteristics and divorced it from the learned behavior of language and culture" (Harrison 52). Social/medical anthropologist Leith Mullings points out that, "Although anthropologists have written extensively about race, anthropological contributions to the study of racism have been surprisingly modest" and notes both the "contradictory heritage" of anthropology and its roots in racial science, acknowledging that the antiracist movement spurred by World War II never became a central tenet of anthropological study (Mullings 669–70). According to Mullings, a disproportionate amount of the antiracist work was done by women, who were often marginalized in the field and by people of color who were either marginalized or excluded from the academy altogether (670). The point Mullings makes about marginalization proves to be true for both Ella and Hurston; the latter studied under Boas at Columbia University.

The 1990s marked some important progress in anthropology: black women gained better recognition in the discipline, and there was a renewed focus on race, particularly through a global lens.[3] Erna Brodber published *Louisiana* during the 1990s. Recognizing the relationship between the increased visibility of black women anthropologists and Brodber's anthropological trope is critical to understanding the black feminist lens with which I interpret the connections between Ella and Hurston in this text. Traditional anthropology has something of a haunting effect on previously colonized people throughout the world. Anthropology's "colonial" reputation conjures visions of spectatorship, exoticization, consumption, and ultimately, exploitation. Such visions might suggest that previously colonized and marginalized groups would find the field of anthropology to be a critical space for revisionist work.

Despite the revisionist potential, even in the post-independence era of postcolonial nations and the post–civil rights era of the United States, anthropology remains a conspicuously white-male-dominated field of study. Moreover, recognizing the paucity of black women in the discipline is critical to understanding the relationship Brodber constructs between *Louisiana* and Zora Neale Hurston. In a cursory history of U.S. anthropology, A. Lynn Bolles explains how it began developing in the 1840s and by the 1880s had become an academic discipline; she emphasizes the paucity of black women in the discipline, revealing that until the 1980s the numbers never moved beyond the low double digits (25). According to Bolles, aside from a general devaluation of black women's work in academe, an additional reason for black women's invisibility in the field is the persistent disdain of "native anthropology"—marginalized people studying themselves.[4] A primary example is Melville Herskovits's insistence that African Americans were unable to be objective enough to conduct fieldwork in Africa, because "they were too close to the cultures" (Bolles 45n). Akhil Gupta and James Ferguson question this continuing prohibitive practice, asking, "Is it merely coincidence that anthropology's boundaries against folklore, ethnic studies, and sociology are constructed in such a way that scholars of color so often fall outside the boundaries of what is considered to be 'real' anthropology?" (30). Although my analysis of race and anthropology began bleakly, Bolles reveals a glimpse of promise when she identifies an increased visibility of black women anthropologists during the 1990s.[5]

Considering the burgeoning presence of black women in anthropology in the 1990s, it is not a coincidence that Erna Brodber published *Louisiana,* a literary narrative grounded in anthropology and folklore, in 1994. Brodber straddles two critical moments for black women scholars

and writers when she positions *Louisiana* in contemporary black feminist anthropological discourse and when she sets the discovery of Ella's
manuscript during the black women writers' literary renaissance in the
United States during the 1970s and continuing into the 1980s.[6] Thus, like
the timing of the publication of the novel, the mysterious delivery of Ella
Townsend-Kohl's manuscript to the editors of the Black World Press in
1974 is also not a coincidence. The editors of the press note, "Its arrival
was well timed, perhaps well planned. Our small black woman's press, like
all other publishing houses was looking for works on and of black women"
(Brodber, *Louisiana* 3); their reaction is indicative of the increased recognition and valuation of black women's cultural productions during this
period. Utilizing these two key points of entry, black feminist anthropology and the black woman's literary canon, Brodber constructs *Louisiana* as
a counter-narrative that challenges anthropological, sociological, and ethnographic research methodologies to represent "truth." Brodber calls into
question how Western thought determines what is real while she interrogates Western constructions of history and productions of knowledge.

Brodber earned an MA in sociology and a PhD in history, the two "sister disciplines" of anthropology. Brodber's efforts to draw cross-cultural
connections between African Americans and Afro-Caribbeans and me-
morialize the legacy of Marcus Garvey resonate with the "racial uplift"
work of many turn-of-the-twentieth-century African American women
in the United States who worked passionately to uplift the race when Re-
construction failed.[7] This resonance stems from what Brodber refers to as
an early race consciousness that made her feel her "business was to serve
[her] race." She elaborates:

My sociological effort and therefore the fiction that serves it, unlike mainstream sociology, has activist intentions: it is about studying the behavior
of and transmitting these findings to the children of people who were put
on ships on the African beaches and woke up from this nightmare to find
themselves on the shores of the New World. It is my hope that this information will be a tool with which the blacks and particularly those of the
diaspora will forge a closer unity and, thus fused, be able to face the rest
of the world more confidently. ("Fiction in the Scientific Procedure" 164)

In *Louisiana,* Brodber's activist intentions are carried out in the field, literally. She uses her classrooms filled with Caribbean social-work students as a space to instruct and to contest dominant discourses, and she accomplishes this work by relying on a Pan-Africanism—the concept of global unity and solidarity between Africans and people of African descent throughout the world—that Irma McClaurin insists is central to the enterprise of black feminist anthropology (9).

Due to its interdisciplinary nature and flexible boundaries, Bolles suggests anthropology is a useful space for black women's counter-narratives or efforts to "set the record straight."[8] Similar to Zora Neale Hurston's valorization and documentation of black folk culture in the southern United States, Brodber utilizes the interdisciplinary nature and flexible boundaries of anthropology as a corrective measure that places value on alternative forms of knowledge. In her essay "Fiction in the Scientific Procedure," Brodber explains that she thinks of herself as a sociologist who employs writing fiction as part of her sociological method. This was particularly true when she wrote her first novel, *Jane and Louisa Will Soon Come Home,* as a case history for students who were offered no Caribbean case studies in their course work. Brodber proposes that those who historically have been doing the research do not share the same concerns or culture as those being researched, and thus, "Accountability has not been to the people researched but to fellow academics." She insists, "the native social scientist cannot operate in this way" ("Fiction in the Scientific Procedure" 166).

Brodber's work strives to give accountability to the people. Her political agenda in *Louisiana* is indeed corrective, as is the agenda of many "native" anthropologists; its greater significance, however, lies in its self-instructive quality. As the "native" anthropologist, Ella enters a new world where she learns a different history, a history that deconstructs master narratives and makes visible diasporic cultural connections. During her instructive apprenticeship with Sue Ann, Lowly, and Madam Marie, Ella not only acquires an alternative view of history but also learns to distrust the laws of so-called science. Under the divine care of this trinity of women, Ella allows herself to embrace the unreal and shirk investments in an irrecoverable past—she "gets over."

HOW ELLA "GOT OVER"

Ella's experience with the venerable sisters results in two initiations: the "transference of souls" (*Louisiana* 38) and "getting over" (97–98). The "transference of souls" occurs when Sue Ann dies and leaves her soul with Ella, thus enabling Sue Ann to communicate with Ella from the dead. The act of transferring Sue Ann's soul, and by extension Lowly's as well, to Ella is described in a manner resembling Vodou spirit possession in which the spirit or *lwa* mounts a person and takes control of her body. Ethnographer and filmmaker Maya Deren explains that the metaphor of *mounting* "is drawn from a horse and his rider and the actions and events which result are the expression of the will of the rider" (29). During the stream-of-consciousness funeral procession that opens *Louisiana*, Sue Ann (also known as "Mammy") and Lowly converse, identifying Ella as their horse:

> "This be the kid?"
> "This is the horse. Will you ride?"
> "Will she do?"
> "Best I have seen. Will you ride?"
> "Let's see if she will." (17)

The transference happens in two parts. First, Ella explains, "By the next morning, November 11th 1936 I was no longer just me. I was theirs. The venerable sisters had married themselves to me—given birth to me, they would say" (32). Early on, Ella recognizes the transference of souls as "a journey into knowing and [that she] was resisting as first timers sometimes do" (38). Her investment in Western constructions of knowledge and history must be dismantled in order for the sisters to use her body as a vessel because the goal of the sisters is, through spirit possession, to offer Ella an alternative form of knowledge that remedies her feelings of loneliness and displacement in the United States.

The second part of this first initiation occurs at Sue Ann's funeral, when Ella shouts out, "Ah who sey Sammy dead," a line from a traditional Jamaican call-and-response song (35). Reuben reveals to Ella that, when she shouted at the funeral, the congregation encircled her, doing "a kind

of shoe patter accompanied by deep grunts" (45) that calmed her into
a faint; Reuben describes it to Ella as a "ring shout." The ring shout has
its roots in Yoruba ceremonial traditions and manifests with slight varia-
tions in the West African–based syncretic religions practiced throughout
the Americas. The ceremonies consist of chanting, drumming, and dancing; the spirit or lwa typically enters the participant once the tempo has
reached its maximum. Ella matter-of-factly comments on this experience,
"I had been officially entered. I was going to be, if I was not already, a vessel, a horse, somebody's talking drum" (46).

The completion of the first initiation, what Ella refers to as her rite of
passage, results in Ella and Reuben moving from Franklin, Louisiana, to
Congo Square in New Orleans. During slavery, slaves gathered at Congo
Square on Sundays to sell produce, dance, sing, and commune. It is also
where Madam Marie Laveau, the infamous Vodou priestess, was rumored
to dance with her snake. During the time in which this narrative is set,
Congo Square had become a central stomping ground for black jazz musicians. It cannot be a coincidence then that Ella and Reuben are sent to
stay with a woman named Madam Marie, who owns a boarding house in
Congo Square and provides psychic healing for West Indian sailors and
travelers who frequent the New Orleans ports. Once in Congo Square, Ella
becomes a "horse" for the venerable sisters to tell their story through, and
for a diasporic assemblage of sailors and travelers who seek their history.

Having been initiated into the realm of the unreal, Ella still has to "get
over" her disinterest in her past and her reliance on Western science in
order to truly perform as the horse or vessel of the venerable sisters. The
idea of someone "getting over" has two meanings, and both are applicable
to Ella's initiation process. "Getting over" or to "get over" on someone is
a concept that has been used throughout the Americas to describe ways
in which both enslaved and free people of African descent have often co-
vertly but sometimes overtly gained some advantage over white people
and white institutions. "Getting over" could be feigning illness or breaking tools to avoid work or, as is the case in *Louisiana,* getting over was
commonplace when slaves syncretized Christianity or Catholicism with
West African religious beliefs unbeknownst to their white overseers. The
key factor in "getting over," then, is that one's act of resistance is never
detected. The Vodou practices that are alluded to in *Louisiana* resulted

from this first concept of getting over. In the context of this text, however, there is also a second form of "getting over," and this form refers to the process that Ella goes through when the venerable sisters teach her a history and epistemological framework that challenge the history and science that have framed her formal, Western education, particularly her studies in anthropology.

The second initiation represents this latter concept of getting over. It is also catalyzed by the singing of lines from the call-and-response song "Ah who sey Sammy dead." Sailors in Madam Marie's parlor sing the song this time. Just as the men sing, "Sammy dead, Sammy dead, Sammy dead oh," Ella's head grows big, her shoulders rock, her body slides from her chair to the floor, and she begins to speak, first as a nine-month-old baby remembering her own Jamaican past, and next as a prophetic oracle, revealing each sailor's past until she tires, exhausted (88–89). This second experience solidifies Ella's purpose—not just her purpose as a "celestial ethnographer" (61) or "soothsayer of the past" (106), but also her need to "give thanks and press on" (93). Ella's getting over is in fact learning how to be at home in the diaspora. Having let go of the past—both the sense of her parents' lost culture and her investment in science—Ella is prepared to examine her life in the present differently. She is ready to embrace a transnational cultural identity and recognize it as something that is full of possibility, rather than representative of loss. Ella's willingness to "give thanks and press on" enables her to claim the field of anthropology as a site of empowerment where, with the assistance of a diasporic community, she can deconstruct Western constructions of history and knowledge. The field of anthropology, then, becomes a space to revise and rewrite the history and culture of people of African descent in the Americas.

THE CURSE OF THE WITCH OF ENDOR AND
THE LOSSES OF FEMALE PROPHETS

New knowledge from the venerable sisters and the steadfast companionship of Reuben get Ella "over," but a significant issue remains—female prophets and barrenness. In a narrative that focuses on the reproduction of knowledge and remembering of obscured or forgotten histories, it would be problematic not to notice that this text is filled with childless women. Experiences as a prophet that are specifically gendered must be examined. Ella's "getting over" is followed by several changes. She stops pressing her hair, begins reading the Bible, becomes a vegetarian, and trades her slacks for loose-fitting, tunic-like dresses. While studying the Bible, Ella discovers a parallel between herself and the story of the Biblical prophet Elijah/Elisha. The connection Ella makes is significant because it helps her to understand her role as a soothsayer of the past.

Ella's conversion takes place in what Madam Marie refers to as "the fullness of time" (98). Ella is initially perplexed by the notion of "the fullness of time" and Madam Marie's assertion that there's another way (99). Unsure of what the "other" way is, Ella proceeds to do things her way, making a parallel between Elijah passing Elisha his mantle and the venerable sisters riding Ella as their horse. Ella is not sure how to interpret this Biblical parallel or the additional Biblical parallel that Sue Ann, Lowly, and she symbolize a holy trinity. It is not until she ponders the difference between Elijah/Elisha, who produced holy prophesies, and the witch of Endor, who is chastised for calling Samuel up from the dead to prophesy for King Saul, that she develops an understanding of Madam Marie's "other" way. Ella's epiphany is that prophets wait for God, which is what Elisha did when he waited for Elijah to pass him his mantle, and what the witch of Endor failed to do when she acted on man's orders instead of God's.

To suggest that the "other" way relies on receiving orders from God is an alternative way of understanding Christianity because, unlike theological interpretations of the witch of Endor where she is condemned for acting as a medium guided by satanic forces, Ella's interpretation does not castigate the witch. Ella's interpretation creates a spiritual space in which African spiritualities and Western Christianity mingle, producing a new syncretic episteme; so, while Madam Marie and Ella's activities conjure Vodou, Brodber complicates diasporic belief systems by syncretizing Vodou, making it a way of life that changes in order to meet the needs of its practitioners. The work that Brodber performs through drawing on and syncretizing Vodou is noteworthy in both the text and in this book. Both *Paradise* and *Louisiana* appropriate Vodou. A form of knowing and foundation for cultural identity formation that appears in multiple texts, Vodou is both a syncretic blending of West African belief systems with Catholicism and a belief system that lends itself to continued syncretizing —a system that is not fixed in time and space.

This analysis of syncretism is significant to my examination of childless women in this text. Lowly dies young and childless. Sue Ann and Silas have children late in life, but the children die. Ella contemplates her seeming barrenness after her first and tenth years of marriage and ponders whether prophets are permitted to have children. Unlike the famed Marie Laveau, who birthed fifteen children and passed her practice on to her daughter and namesake, or Elijah who passed on his prophetship to Elisha, it would seem that Ella is left with no one to pass on her prophetship to. Even the childless venerable sisters give birth to Ella when they pass on the "life-line" (121) to her. The venerable sisters, as well as the West Indian travelers and sailors, literally deplete Ella's energy and strength. By the time she finally pieces together the complete "story," Ella is bedridden and fragile, inflicted by some unidentified, apparently terminal illness. It would seem that Ella is devoured by the needs of the sisters and the men. This intense consumption is yet another lesson for Ella that Reuben assists her in translating. He not only makes the point that they are both too consumed in their own activities to be attentive parents in the traditional sense of biologically reproducing and raising offspring, but he also points out that she has already become a mother: "'What you do is the matrix of many things,' he tells me. It doesn't spell 'mother' though. Nor does it really spell 'horse'" (130). Reuben's revelation enables Ella to understand motherhood outside of patriarchal constructs, just like she understands history, science, and truth outside of Western discourses.

As inviting as it is to read Ella's barrenness as fruitful for the African diaspora and her death as divine, doing so would be shortsighted. In "The Body of the Woman in the Body of the Text: The Novels of Erna Brodber," Denise deCaires Narain argues, "In taking on her role as seer, Ella's sexual presence is de-emphasized and her body represented as the asexual vessel through which the community can find expression and healing. . . . Brodber suggests that the woman's body operates as vessel or vehicle for the powerful delivery of the word which can 'reborn' the black diasporic community" (113–14). This is true. As a mother who births diasporic truths, Ella inverses the conventional production of knowledge and history, a production that is white and male, and instead presents it as black and female. Her inversion, however, raises the question of what is lost in that endeavor. Before Ella "gets over," she makes it a point to mention her powdered sheets that are ever awaiting sexual pleasure: "One thing led to another and another to another much to the delight of the no-longer-sweet-smelling sheets. They clapped their hands for joy" (*Louisiana* 42). These references, which seem somewhat imposed upon the text, are rather bewildering. Aside from seeming misplaced, they would also be highly inappropriate in the 1930s. An unwed man and woman living together would certainly have been stigmatized, especially in a small, rural, southern town; yet, aside from Madam Marie's puzzlement over the bedroom arrangements for Reuben and Ella in her boarding house, no attention is paid to Ella's improprieties.

So, yes, as Narain notes, Ella's sexual presence is de-emphasized as she takes on her role as a seer. Narain, however, does not address the gender component inherent in Brodber's de-sexualization of Ella. The problem is not that Ella does not birth a child who can pass on this diasporic legacy that the sisters reveal to her, because it is convincing that Ella's child, so to speak, is the manuscript that is delivered to the Black World Press. The complication arises from the fact that Ella's personhood and literal life cannot be sustained in her process of becoming. While she is freed from her past, she is quite literally consumed by the past—by the way the past haunts the present, creating all the West Indian men who need her to give them their history. As the men's vessel, her body cannot contain all of their needs and maintain its strength. As the venerable sister's horse, her body is literally ridden to death. Ultimately, Ella experiences a challenge and disappointment that is specifically gendered: the inability to become a mother. Her barrenness is the result of her position as prophet, because her work as a prophet disallows her the opportunity to be a literal mother; mothering a community—its knowledge, history, culture—makes it impossible for her to also mother a family. This is not to say that Ella had an obligation as a woman to produce a biological offspring; rather, the point is that, because of the overwhelming demands of her work, she was not given the *choice* to reproduce.

RE-MEMBERING ZORA

The case of Ella's barrenness, debilitating infirmities, and ultimate death could potentially suggest that what seems to be a libratory text is in fact reaffirming hegemonic and patriarchal values, or at least suggesting that the narrative cannot escape hegemony and patriarchy. Ella's de-sexualization and death can be understood productively if viewed as Brodber's effort to remember the anthropological work of writer, folklorist, anthropologist, and race woman Zora Neale Hurston. Bolles notes that, while significant work has been published on Hurston's literary narratives, little work has been done on her anthropological studies and contributions. Just as Ella becomes a ghostly figure for the Black World Press, who must confirm her existence, Hurston is a ghostly figure in the field of anthropology whose work was devalued and lost until Alice Walker recovered it in the 1970s. Several parallels between Ella and Hurston will exemplify my assertion that *Louisiana*, like Hurston's contributions, exemplifies the fraught relationship between work and pleasure for black women during both the early and late twentieth century.

When selecting Columbia's graduate program in anthropology, Brodber was being quite strategic. Columbia was the institutional home of the prominent anthropologist Franz Boas during the 1930s when Hurston was sent to record the folklore of her hometown, Eatonville, Florida, and when, in *Louisiana*, Ella is sent to collect data in Franklin, Louisiana. Hurston defied the conventions of her times and spent a significant portion of her writing career living in controversy. Hurston was invested in preserving and privileging diasporic folk life during times when such privileging clearly was not in vogue. Her work on folk life in Florida and Louisiana in *Mules and Men* and folk culture in Jamaica and Haiti in *Dust Tracks* were two of many sources of consternation for Hurston. In the introduction to Alice Walker's collection of Hurston's work, *I Love Myself When I Am Laughing . . . and Then Again When I Am Looking Mean and Impressive*, Mary Helen Washington refers to the 1930s as simultaneously Hurston's meridian and the beginning of her "intellectual lynching" (16). Critics during this time wanted images of exploitation and terror— images that Richard Wright and other naturalist writers were apt to produce during the 1940s. Hurston did not believe black writing was obliged to be situated in the mode of racial protest or that her characters must be "tragically colored."[9] According to Washington, "Hurston was determined to write about black life as it existed apart from racism, injustice, Jim Crow—where black people laughed, celebrated, loved, sorrowed, struggled—unconcerned about white people and completely unaware of being 'a problem'" (Intro, *I Love Myself* 17). In other words, Hurston strived to present black people as human first. This desire was reflected in many ways, but one specific way that intersects with Ella's fieldwork is the recording machine, and the parallels and contradictions it creates. When Ella attempts to return the once-valuable, but then-obsolete recording machine to the Anthropology Department at Columbia University, she realizes there was no record of her having it, and no one wanted it. This refusal of ownership is symbolic of the devaluation placed on recording black folk culture; apparently, no one at Columbia registered any value in the ethnographic work produced via the recording machine. While working as an investigator for Carter Woodson at the Association for the Study of Negro Life and History, Hurston expressed a desire to purchase a recording machine "so that she could record what really had happened in black history" (Hemenway 95). In *Louisiana*, Ella unwittingly records with the recording machine "what really had happened in black history," just as Hurston felt the need to do with the machine she desired. The parallel, then, is that Ella and Hurston produced and valued stories that were generally deemed valueless during their lifetime. It is not until the 1970s, when the work of both is rediscovered, that these stories become noteworthy scholarship.

The parallels between Ella and Hurston as black women anthropologists are more apparent than the parallel between Ella's and Reuben's relationship and that of Hurston and men in her life, particularly her husband Herbert Sheen and her friend Langston Hughes. In the foreword to Robert E. Hemenway's biography of Hurston, Alice Walker notes that, though Hurston enjoyed men, she did not need them (xv). Hemenway expounds on this topic when he discusses her brief marriage to Herbert Sheen. Based on her autobiographical accounts in *Dust Tracks*, Hemenway concludes, "two people deeply in love could not share their careers" (94). The sporadic and unconventional career that Hurston embraced simply did not present itself as a strong foundation for a 1920s marriage.

Hurston was convinced that the marriage interfered with her work, and thus felt obliged to chose work over the man whose own mother Hurston claims did not love him as much as she (94). Hurston does not enjoy the companionship that Ella gains from her marriage to Reuben.

While Hurston determined that marriage interfered with her work, Ella's marriage was central to hers. Ella and Reuben complement one another; for both, the success of their own work is contingent upon their involvement in the other's work. As a result of being orphaned and biracial, Reuben constantly feels a sense of unbelonging and displacement. He attempts to cure these feelings through anthropological fieldwork and migration. It is not until he arrives in St. Mary's Parish in Franklin, takes up residence in a village in which the locals insist they already know him, and gives up anthropology in exchange for jazz that he finally possesses a sense of belonging and home. In Ella's words, St. Mary is a homecoming for Reuben:

> Never before in his thirty years had he been a part of the majority. So he was strutting, strumming, learning to jazz and getting acquainted with the blues. Not that he was a total stranger to these two latter, for he had met them in Europe and had ferreted out every music making spot there was in New York. But these products there were processed. In this Louisiana canefield sounds and styles were coming hot out of the oven. He was feeling them in the making, was there at their conception. The man was being made anew. (*Louisiana* 53)

Reuben, like Ella, births diasporic community—her work, which makes diasporic and migratory subjects anew, is intricately connected to Reuben's work with jazz and the blues, musical genres noted for their ability to both express black people's raced experiences and also to provide some degree of solace. Ella's calling to be a prophet ultimately allows Reuben to be homed. Likewise, Reuben plays an important role in Ella's becoming because he understands the interest the venerable sisters have in Ella well before Ella does. After the transference of souls at Sue Ann's funeral, Reuben offers Ella the hypothesis, "Mammy had passed, leaving her soul with me" (38). Reuben's presence and openness to alternative forms of knowledge is critical to Ella's becoming a prophet and to her role as prophet when she falls ill, compelling Reuben to transcribe the manuscript and see that it is delivered to the Black World Press.

Ella's and Reuben's relationship is more than a romantic one. Ella and Reuben function as partners in the sense that each partner's work is invested in the success of the other partner's work. Ella and Reuben offer a striking parallel to Hurston and the poet Langston Hughes. This parallel is important because, as Brodber memorializes Hurston and her work through Ella, she also strives to offer an alternative to the solitude that was ultimately Hurston's existence. Hurston and Hughes established a friendship during the New Negro Movement, also popularly known as the Harlem Renaissance. Their friendship grew into a partnership when they helped organize the quarterly *Fire!!* during the summer of 1926, and they were known to travel together on occasion.[10] It seemed that the partnership would continue to grow when they began co-writing the script of a play, *Mule Bone*. Hurston created the tale, dialogue, and title, while Hughes was to be responsible for the narrative structure and filling out and polishing the language. Hurston felt Hughes betrayed her friendship when he proposed expanding the duties of their typist, Louise Thompson.[11] The relationship eventually ended with attorneys and accusations of theft and dishonesty from both parties.[12] Despite the ugliness of the fallout, both Hurston and Hughes seem to have lamented the bad ending. Hurston reportedly "told the writer Arna Bontemps that she still woke up in the night, crying" over the incident (Rachel Cohen 180). Hughes remembered Zora in "The Blues I'm Playing," a short story in the 1934 collection, *The Ways of White Folk*. The story is about a black pianist who rebels against her white patron and begins playing the blues. Rachel Cohen notes, "the story had the author's tenderness for them all, for the artist, and the manipulative patron, for Hurston and for his younger self . . . and the art they would have made had they stayed friends" (180). The story concludes with the lyrics: "O, if I could holler / Like a mountain jack, / I'd go on up de mountain / And call my baby back" (181). Clearly, both Hurston and Hughes regretted the dissolution of their friendship, though neither ever attempted a resolution.

Although *Louisiana* was published over sixty years after the Hurston-Hughes fallout, the novel itself is set contemporaneously with the fallout. Erna Brodber offers Hurston's and Hughes's relationship resolution. Hurston's work, her anthropological fieldwork in particular, did not afford her the space to sustain her marriage with Sheen. Her working relationship and friendship with Hughes failed as well. Both of these failed relationships suggest that work and pleasure, whether sexual or social, is complicated by gender. This complication can be understood better by turning to Hurston's novel *Their Eyes Were Watching God.*

Since Alice Walker's recovery of *Their Eyes Were Watching God*, as well as her rediscovery of Hurston, many scholars have heralded the novel as a feminist text. Walker's Zora Neale Hurston reader, *I Love Myself When I Am Laughing . . . and Then Again When I Am Looking Mean and Impressive,* is published by the Feminist Press. In the foreword to the 1978 edition of *Their Eyes Were Watching God,* Sherley Anne Williams explains that, after her first encounter with *Their Eyes,* she "became Zora Neale's for life" (vi)—an explanation that speaks to many women's engagement with this text. Despite these claims and the continuing pro-feminist enrapture with Hurston, Mary Helen Washington makes a critical argument that complicates such claims in her 1987 essay, "'I Love the Way Janie Crawford Left Her Husbands': Zora Neale Hurston's Emergent Female Hero," and then again in her 1990 introduction to *Their Eyes.* In the essay, Washington argues, "while feminists have been eager to seize upon this text as an expression of female power, I think it is a novel that represents women's exclusion from power, particularly from the power of oral speech" (*Invented Lives* 237). She notes two scenes in particular where Janie ought to have a voice and does not: when Tea Cake beats her and in the courtroom.[13] Washington explains this paradox of a woman who purportedly has found her voice yet is silent as the conundrum of the questing hero being a woman. In her foreword to *Their Eyes Were Watching God,* Washington notes that during a December 1979 MLA session titled "Traditions and Their Transformations in Afro-American Letters," Alice Walker countered Robert Stepto's assertion of silencing, insisting, "women did not have to speak when men thought they should, that they would choose when and where they wish to speak because while many women *had* found their own voices, they also knew when it was better not to use it" (xii). Similarly, Washington recalls how Michael Awkward later argued that, when Janie tells Pheoby her story, Janie's story becomes a communal one and Janie "is choosing a collective rather than an individual voice" (xii).

Like Washington, I am inclined to remain uncomfortable with Janie's silence at such crucial times. Tea Cake arrives in Janie's life at a time when she is lonely and desiring more than the material possessions her husband left her and more than the communal life that Eatonville offers. Tea Cake literally has nothing to offer Janie other than companionship and a partnership that neither of her husbands would have ever entertained, so I think feminist criticism is fair in arguing that, with Tea Cake, Janie becomes her own person. Nonetheless, "What *Their Eyes* shows us is a woman writer struggling with the problem of the questing hero as a woman and the difficulties in 1937 of giving a woman character such power and such daring" (Washington, Foreword, *Their Eyes* xiv). Hurston is unable to construct a full-fledged partnership between Janie and Tea Cake because of her own inability to fully imagine a voice for Janie. We end up with a writer and a character who possesses no language to demand a partnership—no way of fully imagining such a relationship in 1937. Hurston's limited imagination and Janie's lack of voice should not obscure the novel's remarkable insight. Despite her failures, Hurston recognized the need for a balance between community, kinship, history, and companionship when such a balance was not sustainable.

Brodber addresses voice and partnership in a perplexing manner. In addition to becoming immobile and inexplicably fatigued, Ella nearly loses her voice by the narrative's end. Not only can she not write, she can barely speak either, leaving Reuben the full responsibility of writing/speaking for her. Brodber attempts to downplay this dependency with Sue Ann's insistence and Reuben's eager reiteration that the story is a communal narrative, much like Awkward's explanation of Janie's silence and later storytelling. Sue Ann is insistent that it took herself, Lowly, Silas, Ella, Reuben, Madam Marie, Mrs. Forbes, and the seamen to tell the story. Such an assertion reflects a problematic romantic ideal. I do not believe the communal voice we hear at the conclusion of *Louisiana* effectively celebrates black solidarity and unity. I am also hesitant to interpret the conclusion as some form of tribute to Hurston in which the critic can interpret Ella's silence and ultimate death as libratory. Instead, I would argue that even in 1994 Brodber struggles to locate a space and sustain a partnership that provides her female protagonist the opportunity to experience both work and pleasure—the two become synonymous, prohibiting Ella from attending to her personal needs. I will, however, acknowledge that Brodber constructs a male counterpart who is more appealing and convincing in his interest in a partnership with Ella, as opposed to the constant objectification that Janie remains under even when married to Tea Cake.

These discouraging conclusions are marked by both women's limited choices. Arguably, Ella and Hurston produced fieldwork. Fieldwork in the case of recording and celebrating black culture is certainly a form of reproduction; however, it is a form that falls on the work side of the work-love binary. Ella and Janie are fulfilled characters, and as Hemenway and Walker argue, Hurston found fulfillment in her work. But there is a price. Where are the next generations of "women-warriors" who demand something more—a generation who will continue to pursue and attain both work and love? It is plausible that Ella's mysterious debilitation is a metaphor for the women prophets like Hurston whose work was devalued by the mainstream and often even the marginal culture. It is therefore ironic that Ella's lifeline, which "her men" supposedly help to sustain, withers and leaves her in a state of immobility much like one would imagine Hurston's last days as she died of malnutrition. Even though Reuben assures the readers that Ella did not die in obscurity, just as Walker reveals that Hurston did not either, for both women's funerals are attended in significant numbers, the fact that Brodber saw it fitting to extinguish Ella's life after Ella sustained the lives of men remains troubling.

I have no provocative explanation for the tragic-romantic conclusion Brodber created other than to propose that perhaps both the setting of the text itself and the appropriations of Pan-Africanism and négritude are too romantic. Following Hurston's lead in *Their Eyes Were Watching God*, Brodber sets *Louisiana* in the bayou, a location that shares a type of history similar to that suggested by the muck in which Janie finds temporary security. The bayou and the muck become a safe space, a space outside of the unequal and often brutal realm of white America in the segregated South. According to Donald R. Marks, "Hurston romanticizes the community on the Everglades as a kind of brotherhood that is free of the constraints and class divisions imposed by a mechanistic, capitalistic society like that of Eatonville" (155). As part of the extended Caribbean, Brodber depicts New Orleans as a primal "never-never land" where the African diaspora can meet and revel in its endless continuities. New Orleans is a land where syncretism and transculturation can be observed in every aspect of culture and life. For these reasons, perhaps these seemingly ideal diasporic locations—the Florida muck and the Louisiana bayou—that transcend Eurocentric cultural values and create racially isolated geographies—ultimately foil Hurston's 1937 efforts, as well as Brodber's 1994 efforts.

This does not mean that anthropological fieldwork is not adequate for Ella or Hurston, but it does mean that re-claiming "the field" is a complicated and multifaceted process. By claiming the field of anthropology as a site of empowerment for African diasporic people, Brodber works to liberate diaspora subjects from Eurocentric ideals. Her intervention in Western constructions of knowledge, her troubling of their belief in science, and her emphasis on collective cross-cultural counter-memory is a reconciliatory effort to assist her diasporic readers and students in "getting over" what Brodber describes as "that state in which your body is depressed into physical collapse and something else is activated" (*Louisiana* 98). Her acts of deconstruction and reunification offer her diasporic characters the space to consider the past and their positions in the present differently, or to do as Robert Reid-Pharr encourages, "to imagine life beyond the veil" (13).

Brodber's desire for black people around the world to "get over" effectively reclaims several fields, both the literal geographic locations of black people and the discipline of anthropology. By doing so she reclaims that space for people who have a contested relationship with it. For her characters, the field becomes home. In Gupta's and Ferguson's analysis of "field" and "home," they point out that "'the field' is most appropriately a place that is 'not home'" (13). *Louisiana* serves as a critique of the field of anthropology and of Western constructions of knowledge and history. In doing so, the field most appropriately becomes a place that is home.

As evidenced by Ella's death and her barrenness as well as Hurston's troubled personal and fictitious relationships, home is a messy space. Claiming the field of anthropology as an empowering space for rewriting history and rethinking constructions of knowledge offers Ella, Reuben, and the West Indian sailors' redemption from the past.[14] Such redemption, however, fails to construct a transnational home space that exudes a

critical gender consciousness. In the case of *Louisiana*, critical appropriations of diasporic cultural theories of identity work in two contradictory
ways. The Pan-African ideologies of homogeneity and unity that framed
Marcus Garvey's Universal Negro Improvement Association (UNIA) responded directly to the racial superiority dogma espoused by the philosophers of the European Enlightenment. Garvey and the UNIA propaganda,
however, did not attend to how gender intersects with race. The ideas
about black liberation expressed by Garvey share similarities with other
African-centered liberation movements such as the Pan-African Con-
gresses and post–civil rights black nationalism in their pursuit of freedom through African unity and an emphasis—stated or unstated—on the
position of black men in these efforts. Similarly, the foundational ideology
of négritude of confirming one's being and celebrating blackness fails to
consider the unique challenges gender presents in such acts.

Although Ella is heir to a matrilineal line of black women activists, the
idea that skin, hair, and bone automatically create family and will effectively liberate people of African descent falls flat. The absence of a critical
gender consciousness in the home spaces created in *Louisiana* and *Their
Eyes Were Watching God* is tragic for the female protagonists. Perhaps the
challenge then for black women writers in the twenty-first century is
to build on Hurston and Brodber's vision, creating narratives that not
only make the field a place that is home—because that is important and
necessary—but that also interrogate the interlocking factors of race and
gender in the construction of transnational home spaces. Such imaginings could perhaps make life beyond the veil a more realistic achievement
for black subjects in the United States.

PART TWO

POPULAR CULTURE, TRANSNATIONAL FEMINISM, AND THE LIMITS OF SISTERHOOD

CHAPTER 3

Transnational Sisterhood

Beyoncé and Shakira Sexing the Difference

No matter your race, because you know you're Latino.
—N.O.R.E. (feat. Daddy Yankee and Nina Sky), "Oye Mi Canto"

Where my girls at?
—702

The move away from racialized identity politics in academe is mirrored in popular culture. The music industry, especially through hip-hop and to some degree R&B, is a compelling example of such mirroring. Hip-hop, or at least mainstream representations of the musical element of hip-hop, has evolved into a music genre that is preoccupied with materialism and invested in a capitalist consumer culture. This evolution from its socially conscious roots in rap to its more recent goal of wealth and fame through mass marketing and crossover appeal has spurred spoken-word artist and performer Sarah Jones to rename hip-hop, hip-*pop*. In general, black male hip-hop artists have had more ease and success at appealing to both racially dominant and racially marginalized audiences. Beyoncé Knowles, the reigning queen of pop, however, has managed to finesse the color line, as well as the gender line, rising to international stardom as a performer and more recently as an actress. Her marriage to hip-hop and rap mogul Jay-Z certainly further secures her status.

Just as hip-hop has evolved since its 1970s roots in social protest, so has Beyoncé evolved from Destiny's Child's "daddy's girl"—a marketing that was necessarily directed more at a black audience—to Jay-Z's "Bey," a thinner (especially in the thighs and hips), blonde-haired, lighter-skinned Beyoncé who appeals to an international and interracial audience of men and women. Beyoncé's evolution is fashioned after Berry Gordy's marketing of the Supremes in many ways. Beyoncé's father-manager, Matthew Knowles, arguably decided early on that Destiny's Child would be a crossover group. And just as Dianna Ross eventually pulled away from the Supremes to take center stage, Beyoncé was also destined to be a solo pop icon.

Here I am most interested in Beyoncé's disc *B'Day*, released in 2006, and particularly the re-release of that disc in 2007 with Spanish songs, and the release of the "Beautiful Liar" music-video collaboration with Latina pop icon Shakira. The catalyst for her bilingual album is much more nuanced than simply seeking a stronger crossover appeal. The re-release of *B'Day* with Spanish songs and the collaboration with Shakira is an act of critical appropriation that she hopes will situate her as not simply African American, but as transnational. Early in her career, Matthew Knowles began constructing an image of Beyoncé that emphasized her black bourgeoisie and Creole background, making her a more palatable black woman for white audiences.[1] Her visual transformation since Destiny's Child's debut in the late 1990s therefore makes sense, as does her comment in a Latina.com interview that "I'm just jealous that I wasn't born Latina. I wish I had been because the culture is so beautiful." It is more than the beauty of the culture and more than the dollars that the Latinola market will generate that spurs Beyoncé's regret that she was not born Latina. As Daddy Yankee celebrates in the musical epigraph above, *Latina* is not a race; it is an ethnic group composed of many sub-groups of people from Latin America who can be of any race. Having been born Latina, then, would free Beyoncé from the rigidly constructed racial categorization in the United States that renders her African American or black and not transnational in spite of her self-perceived transnational identity by way of the Creole background she emphasizes. The appropriation of Latinidad on her *B'Day* disc and the production of the "Beautiful Liar" music video with Shakira resists narrow constructions of African American identity. This chapter considers the challenges surrounding black women's collaboration and marketing in the hip-hop music industry as a catalyst for the *B'Day* disc, Beyoncé's rather ingenious collaborations on that disc and with Shakira in the "Beautiful Liar" music video, and whether there are risks when transnational sisterhoods are formed without a praxis that is framed by a critical gender consciousness.

HIP-HOP, LATINIDAD, AND NO ROOM FOR BLACK WOMEN

Collaborations between black, male hip-hop artists and Latina artists and performers are a well-established trend. Hip-hop's intrigue with Latinidad, particularly with what Raquel Rivera refers to as a "butta pecan *mami* fetish," emerged most profoundly in the latter half of the 1990s when hip-hop took a turn from Afrocentric authenticity to ghetto-centricity, or in the case of Latinas, ghetto-tropical (148). While most, if not all, hip-hop–Latinidad collaborations are black male/Latina female, that has not been the case recently. Shakira collaborated with Beyoncé to produce the "Beautiful Liar" track on Beyoncé's *B'Day* disc and to make the music video for the song. This collaboration is significant, because the butta pecan mami fetish that drives the black male/Latina female collaboration reinforces constructions of black females' blackness as undesirable—a construction that reinforces the historical ways in which lightness/whiteness has been privileged in both the white and black entertainment industry. An example of the tension that arises as a result of such color hierarchies is played out in interesting ways in the "Beautiful Liar" music video. Both the *B'Day* album and the "Beautiful Liar" video present a provocative dialectic of competition and alliance and agency and objectification within a transnational paradigm.

The interconnectedness of transnationalism and Latinidad constructs a vexed space for blackness in U.S. popular culture. Cultural studies scholars have critiqued the dangers of homogenization in transnational or post-national perspectives on identity, culture, and political formations that can emerge in transnational discourse. Latina/o scholars have likewise expressed concern with Latinidad as a pan-ethnic construction with a broad demographic frame: "Latinidad describes any person currently living in the United States of Spanish-speaking heritage from more than 30 Caribbean and Latin American countries. It is an imagined community of recent, established and multigenerational immigrants from diverse cultural, linguistic, racial, and economic backgrounds" (Guzmán and Valdivia 207). In spite of their complexities, both of these constructs are currently thriving in academic discourse and in mainstream U.S. popular culture. While I certainly agree with many proponents of transnationalism when they support a shift from U.S.-centric discourse, read as imperialist, to examinations of cultural and political formations outside U.S. borders, I, like many U.S. ethnic studies scholars, believe that this shift is primarily about wanting to be post-race more so than post-nation. In other words, I consistently find that transnationalism provides a space in which scholars and mainstream media can effectively erase the persistence of racism, disenfranchisement, and marginalization of racial minorities within *this* nation. The music industry is a space in which this phenomenon is perpetuated.

During the summer of 2006, I noticed that a significant number of male hip-hop artists were collaborating with non-black, but not-quite-white female artists. Timbaland's and Nelly Furtado's "Promiscuous" and later "Give It To Me," Diddy's and Christina Aguilera's "Tell Me," and Wyclef Jean's and Shakira's "Hips Don't Lie" are several examples. It was not the cross-cultural collaboration that made me uneasy about these collaborations, because I appreciate such work. These particular collaborations struck me as profoundly problematic, because I did not see such crossover collaborations being available to black female hip-hop or R&B artists—unless if you count the Justin Timberlake/Janet Jackson Super Bowl fiasco, which was not a black female/Latino male collaboration. Yes, black female artists consistently collaborate with black male artists, but where are the cross-cultural and interracial collaborations that are available to these male artists?

I sought out other (non-academic) people's perception of this phenomenon, because I wanted affirmation that there was something "shady" about this phenomenon. I was largely unsuccessful in gaining the affirmation, but one response was quite telling. When I explained to my friend's husband that black women do not enjoy the same freedoms to collaborate as do black men in the music industry, he responded rather matter-of-factly, "well, I've never seen a white pimp."[2] The fact that mainstream hip-hop is framed by and celebrates the pimping of women is a well-addressed issue, and thanks to blaxploitation characters and a host of black, male hip-hop artists, *pimp* and *black male* have become analogous terms, despite the existence of white pimps and the profusion of white pimping in the recording industry. This problematic analogy, *pimp* is to *black male* as *respectable* is to *white male*, allows us to see how pimping is (re)produced, and how it consequently places black women in a highly precarious position when it comes to collaborating and hip-hop—their only opportunity to collaborate is when being pimped by black male artists as black male artists mimic how the white music industry pimps black musicians regardless of gender.[3]

This scenario becomes more complicated when the not-quite-white factor of these female collaborators is considered. Aguilera, Shakira, and Furtado reinforce the observation that "We live in an age when Latinidad, the state and process of being, becoming, and/or appearing Latina/o, is the 'It' ethnicity and style in contemporary U.S. mainstream culture" (Guzman & Valdivia 205–6). Aguilera was born in the United States and is of Irish (mother) and Ecuadorian (father) descent. Shakira was born in Colombia and is of Lebanese and Colombian descent. Furtado was born in Canada to parents who emigrated from Portugal. Although being of Portuguese descent is not the same as being of Spanish descent, I include Furtado in this scenario because the Moorish influence in Portugal is one of the main reasons that Portuguese "whiteness" is relative in the Americas, and especially in Latin America.

These women represent Generation E.A. (ethnically ambiguous)—a demographic that advertising executives and fashion magazine editors declare is in high demand: "Today what's ethnically neutral, diverse, or ambiguous has tremendous appeal"; "What is perceived as good, desirable, successful is often a face whose heritage is hard to pin down"; "We're seeing more of a desire for the exotic, left-of-center beauty. . . . [It] represents the new reality of America, which includes considerable mixing. . . . It's the changing face of American beauty" (qtd. in Sharpley-Whiting 30). This demand leaves scholar T. Denean Sharpley-Whiting asking, "Where does, pray tell, such a hierarchy leave Generation Non-E.A. (non-ethnically ambiguous) black women?" (31). It leaves them at the bottom, marked as undesirable and unprofitable artists for crossover collaborations because, as journalist Raquel Rivera points out, "Puerto Rican *mamis* are portrayed most commonly within the hip-hop music realm as a tropical, exotic and racially 'lighter' variation on ghetto blackness, and that is precisely why they are so coveted" (148). Black female music artists, then, become cultural fodder.

Beyoncé, and especially her father-manager, must be acutely aware of the ethnic ambiguity hierarchy that appeals to not only the advertising and fashion industry but also to the hip-hop music industry. Their recognition of how both ethnic ambiguity and transnational collaborations boost consumption and sales is evidenced in Beyoncé's collaboration with Sean Paul on "Baby Boy" for her 2003 disc release of *Dangerously in Love.* Sean Paul is a Jamaican-born dancehall-reggae rap artist who is the embodiment of ethnic ambiguity with one of each of a Sephardic Jewish, Afro-Caribbean, English, and Chinese grandparent. Aside from their video collaboration demonstrating an early effort to position herself and her musical production in a transnational paradigm, the music in the video, Beyoncé's dance choreography, and costume reflect a blending of R&B, dancehall, and Middle Eastern influences. The hybrid production and performance of "Baby Boy" coupled with the popularity of the two performers prompted cultural critic Mark Anthony Neal to label it one of several "high-profile collabos" on the *Dangerously in Love* disc ("Getting Grown"). This high-profile collaboration with Sean Paul and the subsequent collaborations with Latin music stars on *B'Day* symbolize a national phenomenon that writer Danzy Senna satirizes in "Mulatto Millennium" when she mockingly declares, "I thought I'd died and gone to Berkeley. But then I realized. According to the racial zodiac, 2000 is the official Year of the Mulatto. Pure breeds (at least the black ones) are out and hybridity is in. America loves us in all of our half-caste glory" (12).

Knowles's *B'Day* is an impressive yet complicated act of resistance toward the mainstream media and popular culture–driven Latinidad that is portrayed as "that mythical brown race that falls somewhere between Whiteness and Blackness" (Guzman & Valdivia 217). Through her lyrics, collaborations, and self-production of the disc, Knowles insists that the black female body, and specifically her body, is neither marginal nor expendable in the crossover-driven hip-hop industry. While some speculate that her "Irreplaceable" track is a warning to her then boyfriend but now husband, Jay-Z, the chorus line, "You must not know about me," might also be a way of understanding the entire album as a cautioning to the recording industry and the mainstream media that Beyoncé—the pop diva—is irreplaceable. The choices Beyoncé made constructing the reissue package of her *B'Day* disc are provocative despite her ultimately conceding with the familiar adage, "If you can't beat them, join them."

On 3 April 2007, the deluxe edition of *B'Day* was released. It is a two-disc version with five new songs in English and six new Spanish-language songs that include a duet with Alejandro Fernandez and the "Beautiful Liar" duet with Shakira. Adding the Spanish songs is Beyoncé's first act of "joining them," or what I call in this case, a critical appropriation of Latinidad. Shakira, Christina Aguilera, and the Nuyorican queen of pop, Jennifer Lopez, have produced discs in Spanish, while Nelly Furtado has performed several songs in Portuguese. These women's bilingualism not only expands the marketing demographics for their discs, but it also further exoticizes them, separating them from the non-E.A. black woman whose blackness and typical monolingualism limits her appeal. By adding the Spanish-language songs, Beyoncé not only expands her market but inserts herself into the Latinidad media craze.

Collaborating with the Latin Grammy–winning Mexican pop singer Alejandro Fernandez is obviously a savvy and lucrative marketing strategy. The fact that the ballad "Amor Gitano" was written for the Latin soap opera *El Zorro: La Espada y la Rosa* makes the collaboration even savvier because the popularity of telenovelas in Latin pop culture guarantees that Beyoncé infiltrates the Latin market. In addition to the monetary gain, which of course is the goal of most artists, this collaboration has a more significant marketing value. Beyoncé is collaborating with a non-black male, breaking a crossover barrier that her black female vocal counterparts have not been as successful at and black male singers have done with ease. In addition to the cross-cultural element of her crossover, the song itself is critical to marketing Beyoncé. "Amor Gitano" translates in Spanish as "gypsy love."[4] The female vocalist lines, which Beyoncé co-wrote, promise unfaltering love and that she will follow her lover wherever he goes.[5] The ballad is set to flamenco rhythms with guitar accompaniments and a subdued pop beat.

This is not the typical Beyoncé hollering about how sexy her body is, materialistic pursuits, or the betrayal that scholar Daphne Brooks refers to as the anthem of black women's R&B productions during the 1990s.[6] Instead, we hear a soft, passionate performance that counters the angry-black-woman/over-sexed-black-woman image that reinforces popular constructions of black women as undesirable. When scholar bell hooks discusses representation of black female sexuality, she contends that black women are deemed "[u]ndesirable in the conventional sense, which defines beauty and sexuality as desirable only to the extent that it is idealized and unattainable," whereas "the black female body gains attention only when it is synonymous with accessibility, availability, when it is sexually deviant" (hooks, *Black Look*, 65–66). In this ballad Beyoncé presents a reformed persona that clearly is palatable cross-culturally, considering the single peaked at number one on the Spanish singles chart and at number thirty-eight on the Mexican chart. That the lyrics are in no way sexually explicit, but instead are ruminations on romance, sunshine, and destiny—ideas appropriate to ballads—clearly set Beyoncé outside of the "sexually deviant" black female body that bell hooks insists is the only persona through which the black female body gains attention.[7]

Collaborating with Fernandez on "Amor Gitano" demonstrates how one particular Generation non-E.A. black woman has infiltrated the ethnically ambiguous hierarchy, and does it in a manner that defies standard depictions of black female sexuality. Beyoncé does not use this approach in her collaboration with Shakira, however. She returns to the sexual deviance that maintains her status as an international sex icon, but this collaboration nonetheless has a provocative intellectual component. If black women are not "hot," because they are not "paprika'd and salted with difference," then through the "Beautiful Liar" collaboration, Beyoncé appropriates the difference that makes Generation E.A. "hot" and palatable. But before discussing how she appropriates these differences, it is useful to first discuss the significance of collaborating with Shakira.

Singer-songwriter Shakira Isabel Mebarak Ripoll was born in Barranquilla, Colombia, to a New York–born father of Lebanese descent and a mother of Catalonian parentage. She immigrated to the United States in the late 1990s in order to work with Emilio and Gloria Estefan in Miami. Having lived in the port city of Barranquilla, Shakira was influenced by many styles of music, which has heightened her success at being marketed to diverse U.S. audiences. Her eclectic musical repertoire coupled with her myriad linguistic influences—she has recorded albums in Spanish, English, Portuguese, and Arabic—reflect the moniker of "idealized, transnational citizen" that scholar Maria Elena Cepeda aptly uses to discuss how Shakira is portrayed in mainstream U.S. culture. Shakira's knack for incorporating belly dance, or what the media often calls "hip shaking," into her dance performances enhances her already well-established transnational persona. Her hip shaking has won her acclaim at such venues as the 2006 closing ceremony at the World Cup in Berlin, the 2007 Grammy Awards in the United States, and at her *Oral Fixation* concert in Mumbai. Prior to her collaboration with Beyoncé—the collaboration was a winwin for both women—perhaps Shakira's biggest move toward expanding her market in the United States was when she collaborated with Haitian American rapper Wyclef Jean on "Hips Don't Lie."

"Hips Don't Lie" topped charts around the world, and according to Media Traffic it is the second most successful single behind Cher's 1999 "Believe."[8] This performance and music video for this song, as the title suggests, demands that the viewer become fixated with Shakira's hips and with the rest of her body as she belly dances across the stage. Shakira's hips catapulted this track to international fame. And the montage of rap with reggaeton and Middle Eastern beats, belly dancing, and the Lebanese-Colombian and Haitian-U.S. personas of Shakira and Wyclef solidified it as the embodiment of transnational, global music. This is what Beyoncé banks on when she collaborates with Shakira.

Beyoncé banked well on the "Beautiful Liar" collaboration. According to Billboard.com the single moved from number ninety-four to number three in an unheard-of leap the week of 7 April 2007, its second week on the Billboard Hot 100 chart. Beyoncé accomplished two critical things with this collaboration, just as she did with Fernandez. She once again gained access to both the U.S. Latina/o and the Latin American fan base, reinforcing her already global appeal. A global appeal and a transnational persona, however, are not synonymous. Beyoncé is recognized around the world as a hip-hop/R&B artist; thus she is always already read as black, not transnational. Working with Shakira and learning how to belly dance and singing a Spanish-language duet with Fernandez add a transnational dimension to Beyoncé's persona that does much more than simply increase her sales—it transforms her blackness. The Spanish-singing, belly-dancing Beyoncé becomes more difficult to simply categorize as black hip-hop or R&B singer—or *unsalted* and without difference. Newly paprika'd and crossing over into Latinidad, Beyoncé would seem undefeatable in mainstream popular culture.

I am sure Beyoncé will maintain her appeal for some time to come, but alas, it cannot be this simple: black, female hip-hop singer infiltrates hip-hop–Latinidad collaborations. In order for Beyoncé to be read as transnational, she must not be read as African American. The manipulation of her phenotype has been central to Beyoncé's construction of a transnational identity that trumps, if not negates, her African American identity. Although skin color is not the controlling factor in being a transnational commodity, it is nonetheless a particularly important factor in the economics of race, especially for black women in the entertainment industry. The reality of the privileging of gendered whiteness in the entertainment industry is evidenced in visual transitions Beyoncé undertook since her debut with *Destiny's Child.* Well before *Radar* magazine accused *Vanity Fair* of lightening Beyoncé's skin to increase newsstand sales of their October 2005 issue featuring her on the cover, Beyoncé Knowles had already begun a "bleaching" process that would make her more marketable to mainstream audiences.[9] When describing the "bleaching" phenomenon among Latina pop singers Jennifer Lopez, Christina Aguilera, and Shakira, Maria Elena Cepeda notes that, since these women's "respective emergence onto the US market, each woman has grown successively thinner and blonder with time . . . in essence manipulating the visual in a way that renders them more 'user-friendly' to non-Latinos" (221). Beyoncé has certainly become more "user-friendly" since her debut in the music world in the quartet Destiny's Child.[10] For starters, she quickly ditched the corn-rowed extensions that she donned on the cover of the 1999 release of Destiny Child's *Writing on the Wall* album. Since then, her extensions have become progressively blonder and no longer display the ethnic looking braids. In photos with fellow group members Kelly Rowland and Michelle Williams, the significantly lighter Beyoncé is consistently positioned in the middle of the trio, thus enhancing her lightness.

Ironically, Ruth La Ferla's "Generation E.A.: Ethnically Ambiguous" *New York Times* article notes that Beyoncé "sometimes wears her hair blond" as an example of megastars masquerading as racial hybrids. *The Observer* makes a similar point: "Not surprisingly, pop stars —always alert to shifting fashions —are playing with ethnic ambiguity. Beyoncé, a black American, often wears her hair blond."[11] Perhaps these suggestions that Beyoncé's blonde hair produces ethnic ambiguity is influenced by Tina Knowles, Beyoncé's mother, responding to a query about her own ethnic and regional background: "I was born in Galveston, Tex., of French and Cherokee Indian descent," forgetting her [dominant] African heritage.[12] Not surprisingly, Beyoncé expresses a similar flippancy about her own ethnicity in a *Newsweek* roundtable. Asked about black women's beauty and how it is perceived and portrayed, Beyoncé responds, "Well, I could complain about being light-skinned. But that's life. People judge you by the way you look, unfortunately, before they speak to you."[13] In addition to an investment in an ethnic ambiguity that erases blackness, Beyoncé has also become noticeably thinner, particularly in the hips and thighs. In fact, she lost twenty pounds in 2006 for her role in the film *Dreamgirls*. The transformation apparently worked, because in the askmen.com Top 99 Most Desirable Women poll, Beyoncé moved from number fifty in 2006 to number one in 2007, beating number-seven-ranked Shakira.

MOCK FEMINISM OR THE "REAL" DEAL

While Beyoncé transcends significant barriers for African American women positioning themselves as subjects in transnational discourse, her political agency is a complicated act. In "Suga Mama, Politicized," a review article in *The Nation,* Daphne A. Brooks proclaims that *B'Day* is "one of the oddest, most urgent, dissonant and disruptive R&B releases in recent memory." She goes on to insist, "It comes at a time when public and political voices of black female discontent remain muted and mediated in the public eye," making connections between this album and the disproportionate number of black women left homeless after Hurricane Katrina. Brooks performs an interesting, but unconvincing, critique of how Beyoncé inserts a social consciousness into this album that "challenges century-old American myths about race, class and gender." While I agree with Brooks's argument that some of the tracks counter the myths "that still portray black women as lazy, feckless, 'degenerate' and unwilling to work," the images that replace the common stereotypes are not particularly revolutionary. I am not confident that replacing "gold digger" images of black women—lazy, feckless, degenerate and unwilling to work—with images of black woman as "suga mamas" is progressive. Beyoncé's shift from wanting a man who can pay her "bills, bills, bills"[14] to being pleased to have a man who is happy to let her "take care of mine" does not demonstrate how the "album of hard, militarized beats marches in defiance of a long history of public black women . . . who have been stripped and stressed and displaced and denied" (Brooks). Instead, I see these tracks lending credence to popular images of black women as everything from erratic spurned lovers—think *Waiting to Exhale* drama and Angela Bassett setting her philandering husband's BMW on fire—to materially driven gold diggers à la Kanye West's song "Gold Digger." I am not denying that the highly raced and gendered public images of black women do not influence Beyoncé's lyrics; I am certain they do. What I am saying is that the political agency and even the critical thought on Beyoncé's part that Brooks argues for in her assessment come across as romanticized.

In spite of my skepticism regarding the song lyrics, I will concede Brooks's argument about Beyoncé becoming a production Svengali. It is ironic that Beyoncé recorded this album in two weeks, just after shooting the film *Dreamgirls*. The irony is that, in her role as Deena in *Dreamgirls*, Beyoncé is the female pop star who has no control over her sound, what she produces, or how she is marketed. Even when she takes action to attempt to resist patriarchy, Deena finds patriarchy inescapable until she combines agency with sisterhood. With this album, Beyoncé has done that, even if only to a small degree. In addition to proposing a transnational sisterhood with Shakira, Beyoncé took control of her sound, production, and marketing. She orchestrated the recording in secret from her father/manager and Columbia Records. She also selected her production staff, decided how the producers would work together, and she co-wrote and co-produced all of the songs. Brooks reveals how these actions of agency and control are not typical: "Whether you believe it or not, this is a rather unique and remarkable spin story for a female R&B artist's album: Everyone from Mariah Carey to Mary J. Blige to Christina Aguilera has aggressively centered the making of their recordings (and their success) around a producer." In this regard, then, I do agree with Brooks that Beyoncé is unquestionably well aware of her own raced and gendered position in U.S. culture and demonstrates a particular type of agency.

Regardless of whether Beyoncé should be credited with a strong sense of agency on the original release that Brooks reviews, the image changes and collaborations that are made on the deluxe edition of *B'Day* are brilliant from a marketing perspective. Beyoncé collaborates with Shakira to produce the "Beautiful Liar" track and to make the music video for the song. The butta-pecan-mami fetish that drives the more common black male/Latina female collaborations reinforces constructions of black females as undesirable, as when Wyclef insists that Shakira's hips "make a man wanna speak Spanish,"[15] and when Snoop Dogg's "Black and beautiful, you the one I'm choosin' / Hair long and black and curly like you're Cuban" lyrics emphasize a hybrid blackness as the ideal beauty.[16] So then, while Latina *mamis* are sexualized and objectified just as problematically as black women are in hip-hop culture, they are also portrayed "as a tropical, exotic and racially 'lighter' variation on ghetto blackness, and that is precisely why they are so coveted" (Rivera 148). Such portrayals are troubling in two ways. They fail to register that *Latina* is not a race and that the ethnic identity is composed of people who span a full black-white color spectrum—all Latinas are not "a tropical, exotic and racially 'lighter' variation on ghetto blackness." Furthermore, the portrayals subordinate the African American female body and inevitably create a tension between Latina and African American women.[17] I distinguish between "African American" and "black" here because there are black Latinas in the United States. This tension, however, may be resolved if we consider the lyrics of "Beautiful Liar" in addition to its images. Analyzing the lyrics and the images reveals how both women are subjects of patriarchy and its manipulation of racial and sexual difference, thus making Beyoncé and Shakira become alike not only socially but also visually.

Lyrically the "Beautiful Liar" track lacks originality as it delves into the same-old-same-old of spurned lover and the other woman. The song is about two women who realize they are involved with the same man, and they decide he is not worth a fight. How the choreography intersects with the lyrics transforms a stale trope into an interesting discourse on transnational feminism and the uses of the erotic. According to Beyoncé, the song, like the album, is invested in female empowerment and solidarity. The choreography adds a provocative dimension to the trope. The video opens with Middle Eastern wind instruments and moaning and the silhouettes of Beyoncé and Shakira masked by dry ice. Both women are dressed in black with long, wind-blown tresses. As the dry ice dissipates, the camera quickly pans back and forth from one woman to the other with few close-up shots, ultimately making it difficult to distinguish one from the other. It is not until immediately before the bridge that both women are shown in the same shot. It is at this point that the video becomes interesting, and perhaps lends some credence to efforts by Brooks to depict *B'Day* as a politically and socially conscious album in her review.

Just before the bridge, both Beyoncé and Shakira are shot lying head to head on the floor, singing and gyrating, one of Beyoncé's favorite movements in videos. At the bridge, they roll to their bellies and rise to their feet as the wind instruments become dominant again. Once on their feet they perform a belly dance in front of a wall covered with characters from the ancient Iranian language Avestan. The staging shifts back and forth from the wall to the women dancing in the rain. The wall scenes become increasingly erotic, as the women dance against the wall in unison, making their bodies buck and grind against the wall. The video ends with Beyoncé facing the wall, hands pressed against it, legs extended behind her in a walking stride, as she rocks her hips backward and forward toward the wall. Shakira is within arm's reach of her with her back against the wall, arms raised above her head as though they are bound.

Having discovered the lover's infidelity, the chorus is a composition of both women agreeing not to "kill the karma," because a "beautiful liar" is not worth fighting and drama. They agree the better alternative is to "live without him," because he is nothing more than a beautiful liar. The chorus is where Beyoncé intersects with public and political voices of black female discontent—not when she talks about setting fires as Brooks suggests in her review. Beyoncé draws on the trope of sisterhood that has been a dominant sustainer in black women's fiction. Toni Morrison's novels *Sula, Paradise,* and *Love,* for example, present strong examples of women who realize, albeit often belatedly, that heterosexual relationships prohibit female bonding that would have sustained and nurtured the women. Thus, as Anissa Janine Wardi proposes about the female protagonists in Morrison's *Love,* the same holds true for Beyoncé and Shakira: "their strongest desire is for one another, not the men" (213). At the finale of the composition, the two women resolve that the beautiful liar is the one to blame rather than one another. Shakira expresses her sense of shame and Beyoncé laments her inability to free Shakira from her hurt and pain.

Calling out the impropriety of the man and determining "We can live without him" contrasts starkly with the position that the trio 702 takes in the song "Where My Girls At." This song was composed by TLC's Lisa "Left Eye" Lopes and produced by Missy Elliott. Instead of determining that a player is not worth her time, the lead vocalist of "Where My Girls At" identifies the male object of desire as "property" and in a hard ghetto-centric yet sexy way warns any potential poachers not to "violate" her by trying to take her man, or she will "Chop you down to size."

If this is not warning enough, the hook reminds potential poachers that her girls have her back each time she asks, "Where my girls at" and her girls flank her on the left and right throughout the music video. My purpose in contrasting these two performances of sisterhood is not to cast judgment on the former being progressive and the latter representing re-gressive gender politics. It is to demonstrate how Beyoncé has flipped a rather trite conception of hard, angry black women who do things like "bust the windows out your car"[18] or "hit 'em up style / put your hands in his cash"[19] and presents a black womanhood that is thoughtful, inde-pendent, and able to produce her own pleasure. These attributes alone obviously are not what will position black women as being understood as embodying transnational sensibilities, but these attributes do disrupt particular types of images that cast African American women in a strictly nationalist role, failing to recognize how their position in a nation within a nation produces transnational identity formations without their cross-ing national boundaries. Furthermore, the choice that Beyoncé's and Sha-kira's personas take when they choose a strength that they perceive being produced by their own alliance instead of threatening to "chop you down to size" privileges a different kind of sisterhood than the angry-payback-*sistah*hood that is popular in black women's rap and R&B lyrics. Beyoncé's and Shakira's creation of a sisterly solidarity across national, racial, and cultural lines positions Beyoncé much differently from 702.

When read together, the distinctive difference of the solidarity of "Beautiful Liar" suggests that both of the spurned women can gain plea-sure and vindication by reconciling with and trying to help one another heal. Beyoncé's and Shakira's wall dancing that invokes a lesbian erotica is clearly staged for the male viewer's pleasure, or at least, that is likely to be the mainstream interpretation of it. If one views the wall dancing through a transnational feminist lens, however, the erotic becomes the empowering "resource" Audre Lorde insists is "within each of us that lies in a deeply female and spiritual plane, firmly rooted in the power of our unexpressed or unrecognized feelings" (53). One could then interpret the highly erotic post-bridge performance and the insistence that "we can live without him" as the women becoming in touch with the erotic and becoming less willing to accept powerlessness. The erotic in this video reinvents transnational sisterhood as a normal and ancient practice with the inclusion of the Avestan characters as backdrop to the centuries-old Middle Eastern dance. The video suggests that transnational feminism or sisterhood is a return to long-forgotten roots, to a natural order of things that patriarchy stole from women. If examining gender alone, this brand of feminism seems empowering, but how race, ethnicity, and cultural identity intersect with gender will once again complicate the issue.

"Beautiful Liar" provides an interesting dialectic of competition and alliance and agency and objectification within a transnational paradigm. The Latinidad that Shakira embodies represents a clear challenge for Beyoncé to overcome in a music industry that privileges female whiteness. Yet Shakira also becomes an ideal, female collaborator as a result of the very essence of their competition. And Beyoncé is likewise an ideal collaborator for the Latin pop/rock singer who has achieved international fame, but has not tapped nearly as many social economies as Beyoncé. The dialectic of agency and objectification becomes a difficult hurdle to leap, though. The nature of their transnational sisterhood and their use of the erotic is rooted in orientalism. In this video Beyoncé and Shakira appropriate belly dance in much the same way that the late 1960s and 1970s women's movement claimed it as a symbol and performance that challenged "prior Western conceptions of the female body as negative" (Shay and Sellers-Young 16). The women's movement's intrigue with belly dance was informed by nineteenth-century Western condemnations of the dances of traditional Middle Eastern and North African women "as gratuitous sexual display, fetishised into a sign of the 'Orient's' sensuality and abandon, deemed grotesque, and immoral, censored and all together banned" (Keft-Kennedy 280). "In the beginnings of the 'belly dance movement,'" dance scholars Anthony Shay and Barbara Sellers-Young explain, "this once unacceptable presentation of the female body became a powerful means of transcendence as a group of women decided to redefine the belly dance as a symbol of personal and sexual liberation" (17).

Beyoncé and Shakira employ belly dance as an act of agency like the second-wavers in the women's movement. Although belly dance is used in this video as an empowering (erotic) resource that "lessens the threat of [our] difference" (56), as Lorde insists, and in turn overcome the nagging dialectic of agency and objectification, it is nonetheless problematic. "The images projected by Westerners in the performance of belly dance and other forms of oriental dance," according to Shay and Sellers-Young, "raise the thorny issue of orientalism. The vocabulary of the dance and its position within the framework of the West, especially the United States, as 'other' provide an 'empty' location, as in 'not part of my culture' for the construction of exotic new fantasy identities" (14). The thorny issue of orientalism draws attention to the insinuation that when the women come together to reject their pimping by a beautiful liar, race and ethnicity are rendered irrelevant, because the beautiful liar is a male, as though only gender matters. The video ultimately attempts to forge a raceless sisterhood that coheres around patriarchy, and thus raises many critical questions about the intersections between race, ethnicity, gender, and transnationalism.

A contradiction would seem to emerge when the video suggests that the erotic is an empowering source that forges a gendered transnational solidarity between African American and Latina women, and yet these very women perform orientalism in a manner that reinforces problematic Western caricatures of Eastern cultures. Similar to my conclusion about the failure for women to experience both work and pleasure in *Louisiana,* I have no simple conclusion to sum up the contradictions inherent in Beyoncé's politics and appropriations. When, however, one considers the ways in which third-wave feminism has been unwilling or uninterested in rigid and constant definitions of feminism, there is perhaps a way to understand the seemingly uncritical performance of orientalism in "Beautiful Liar" as something more than thoughtless.

Considering how third-wave feminism could potentially influence the choice to incorporate an orientalist element in the video provides a sort of unconscious reasoning for the orientalism that supports claims of social consciousness by Brooks. And, while I will not go so far as to impose a particular brand of feminism on Beyoncé, because feminism is a conscious social and political project, I will argue that the social and gender consciousness reflected in the "Beautiful Liar" video exudes a third-wave essence. Third-wave feminism is consistently noted for its complexity and privileging of pluralities. According to Amber Kinser, contradictions are "[a] recurrent and resounding theme in third-wave literature." Kinser draws on Cathryn Bailey when she suggests, "[p]art of the rhetorical significance of the third wave is that it can help us learn . . . 'to live more comfortably with ambiguity and contradiction,' and learn that 'complexity, multiplicity, and contradiction can enrich our identities as individual feminists and the movement as a whole'" (139). The seeming contradiction of what can come across as an uncritical orientalist element in the video can also be read as an example of the contradictions that embody a new wave of feminism that feels no obligation to be bound by rigid definitions and guidelines for what a feminist "looks" like—as the t-shirts say—or how a feminist thinks or behaves.

Beyoncé shares interesting and, perhaps, unexpected viewpoints with the women and men who contributed to Rebecca Walker's third-wave anthology *To Be Real*. Walker insists neither she nor the contributors to the collection have "bowed out," but rather, they have refused to subscribe to any particular ideal and have instead chosen to "be real" and tell the truth (qtd. in Henry 150). The review of the *B'Day* disc by Brooks in the *Nation* attends to this notion of "being real" when Brooks argues there is an explicit social consciousness in the production and performance. My critique of the transnational politics at play in both the disc and the music video speak to the "telling the truth" aspect that Walker says frames the contributions to her collection. What becomes evident, then, is something Kimberly Springer points out about young black women who continue to do "feminist analyses of Black life, but they are not necessarily claiming the label of *third wave*" (1060). Although it is not likely that Beyoncé will ever identify herself as a third-wave feminist, the influence of third-wave feminism—whether there consciously or unconsciously—can be seen in her cultural productions. These productions register the "more" that Lone DuPres insists folk sometimes need in *Paradise*. Black women, and specifically African American women, need a space where both a critical gender consciousness and a transnational consciousness convene, a place where complexity, plurality, and ambiguity commingle in a sometimes messy but ultimately fulfilling way. Through their critical appropriation of Latinidad and performance of orientalism, the *B-Day* disc and the "Beautiful Liar" video create the space "just yonder" that Piedade promised the Convent women would free them from the evils that haunted their lives.

THIRD WAVE FEMINISM, PARADIGM SHIFTS, AND BLACK MASCULINITY

CHAPTER 4

He Said Nothing

Brasilidade and Aphasia in Danzy Senna's *Caucasia*
and Gayl Jones's *Corregidora*

I n Part One, I discussed the challenges that gender poses in efforts to
position African American women's cultural productions in a transnational framework. The critical appropriations performed in *Paradise* and *Louisiana* enable African American women who do not travel
the ability to develop and embrace a transnational identity. The benefit
of the appropriations, however, is complicated by gender; nearly all of
the women die. My analysis in Part Two takes into consideration the dilemma of death that accompanies embracing transnational identities in
Paradise and *Louisiana*. Beyoncé Knowles's performances on her *B-Day*
disc and particularly her collaboration with Shakira call into question
ideas of family genealogy, kinship, and black community that have pre-
vailed in African American women's cultural productions. In Beyoncé's
performances these tropes are replaced with the idea of a transnational
sisterhood that not only positions African American women at the center
of transnational discourse, but that also could potentially be a tool to allow African American women to distance themselves and their work from
the periphery of black cultural discourse. However, similar to Morrison
and Brodber, Knowles does not do the self-reflective work of considering
what the pitfalls can be when appropriating diasporic theories of cultural
identity. This final section focuses on Danzy Senna's *Caucasia* and Kasi
Lemmons's *Eve's Bayou*, a novel and a film that consider the pitfalls of
critical appropriations and avoid using death or sisterhood as convenient
"escape hatches" for dealing with gender differences. Senna and Lemmons are more successful at producing a critical gender consciousness, as
well as locating a safe home space for African American women, because
they deconstruct the tropes of family, kinship, and community that frame

the cultural productions of Brodber, Morrison, and many other African American women artists.

This chapter moves in a different direction from the previous three that focused heavily on African Americans embracing transnational identities. Here I consider how critical appropriations of *Brasilidade* (Brazilianness) in Danzy Senna's *Caucasia* operate as a warning about the potential pitfalls of uncritical appropriations. The approach I use for analyzing the potential pitfalls is an examination of the father-daughter relationship in the novel and the silence that surrounds it. While much attention in African American literary criticism has been devoted to African American women's silence, significant attention has not been directed to African American men's silence, as opposed to their action, which is an often-acknowledged characteristic of the African American male quest for freedom and subjectivity. The silence that circumscribes the father-daughter relationship in *Caucasia* is intricately linked to the critical appropriation of Brasilidade, a paradigm of national identity and racial formation. Brasilidade can be understood as the Brazilian post-slavery effort to position itself as a modern nation by defining a national identity that resists foreign influences, particularly by rejecting European culture and instead embracing African and indigenous ancestry and culture. In the process of privileging cultural hybridity, racial mixture inevitably is celebrated as a unique and distinguishing component of Brazilian national identity. The contradiction inherent in the rhetoric of Brasilidade is that African-descended people in Brazil were not and continue not to be fully incorporated citizens who experience the same rights and privileges as those who are considered white in Brazil.

Although my analysis focuses primarily on *Caucasia*, I draw on Gayl Jones's *Corregidora* in order to consider how the false propaganda of racial democracy and black incorporation into the nation perpetuated by Brasilidade extended across hemispheres to the African American imagination in the United States. I argue that such propaganda produces a metaphorical aphasia in the fathers in both *Caucasia* and *Corregidora*. The term *aphasia* is apropos because, just as the false propaganda of Brazilian racial democracy silenced Afro-Brazilians and worked toward erasing blackness, when that propaganda travels to the United States it manifests as a disease that silences Martin in *Corregidora* and Deck in *Caucasia*. *Cor-*

regidora provides a framework for analyzing the appropriation of Brasilidade, silence, and the father-daughter relationship in *Caucasia*, because *Corregidora* provides both a textual and historical example of how when transplanted in the United States the racial ideals of Brazil's racial democracy wreak havoc on the African American family. In an act that perhaps responds to the troubles produced by privileging Brazilianness rhetoric in *Corregidora*, *Caucasia* critically examines this appropriation and offers an insightful paradigm shift around notions of family, kinship, and community that both produces a transnational narrative without privileging travel while also avoiding death and sisterhood as the only means for African American women to negotiate the complexities of hybrid cultural identities.

GEOGRAPHIES OF FREEDOM AND BRAZILIAN MODERNISM

By nature of their forced transportation to and enslavement in the United States, African Americans have a long history of imagining what I call *geographies of freedom*. During and immediately after slavery these geographies were often the northern states and, to a lesser degree, western states and territories. Immediately upon being transported to the Americas and even in the contemporary era, however, a return to Africa, the lost motherland, has also been a central geography in the imaginings of freedom. In African American cultural studies, Brazil has received less critical attention than Africa and various U.S. regions as a geography of freedom. The social theories and political praxis that frames the construction of Brazilian identity formation during the first half of the twentieth century make Brazil an important hemispheric influence on transnational identity formations in U.S. literature throughout the twentieth century. A detailed understanding of Brazil's social history is unnecessary here, but a brief overview is warranted in order to understand the hemispheric relationship between Brazilian social theories and the transnational identity formations that produce the silence in *Corregidora* and *Caucasia*.

At the beginning of the twentieth century, Brazil was confronted with the white supremacy of scientific racism and with its own insecurities as a neocolonial nation. During the trans-Atlantic slave trade, more than eleven times the number of slaves transported to the United States were transported to Brazil, resulting in a far greater percentage of Brazilians with African rather than European or Amerindian ancestry when African slavery was abolished in 1888. In light of the beliefs of white supremacy and the racial hierarchies espoused in European and American pseudo-science, Brazilians initially felt embarrassed by the undeniable racial mixture that framed the colonial history of Brazil. The Brazilian modernist movement during the 1920s and 1930s offered Brazilians an alternative framework for understanding their cultural and social history—a framework that evoked pride instead of shame. There are two main components to Brazilian modernism, the social theory and political praxis element and the literary and cultural one.

In contrast to the anti-miscegenation laws that were at the heart of significant racial violence in the United States during the first half of the twentieth century, Brazil encouraged miscegenation. They encouraged it under the eugenicist premise that through interracial marriage, within one hundred years or five generations, all elements of blackness would be "absorbed" and Brazil would be a white or mostly white nation. Describing what he calls "the whitening thesis," Thomas E. Skidmore explains that between 1889 and 1914 "the whitening thesis offered Brazilians a rationale for what they believed was *already* happening. They borrowed racist theory from Europe and then discarded two of that theory's principal assumptions—the innateness of racial differences and the degeneracy of mixed bloods—in order to formulate their own solution to the 'Negro Problem'" (77). This sort of reverse eugenics model that encouraged reproduction with undesirable groups in order to produce an ideal, "whitened" species fueled Brazil's advertisements in North American and European newspapers, enticing white immigrants to settle in Brazil and "mix eventually with the native population, thereby diluting Brazil's large black population" (Telles 29).

No political discourse was nearly as effective at triumphing the whitening ideology as sociologist Gilberto Freyre's 1933 publication of *The Masters and the Slaves* (Casa Grande e Senzala). By privileging what political scientist Michael Hanchard refers to as "Luso-tropicalism," Freyre conceptualized a theory of "racial democracy." This ideology refutes theories of scientific racism purporting miscegenation to be damaging to the nation and claims that people of African descent were biologically inferior were also refuted. Like various other Latin American intellectuals who sought to refute racial science theory, Freyre emphasized culture over biology and celebrated those differences while "equat[ing] miscegenation with the subsequent civic equality of racially distinct groups and the fusion of indigenous, European, and African 'races' into a superior, brown-skinned, mulatto nation" (Hanchard 4). It was in this same fashion that a modernist literary and art movement headed by Oswald de Andrade and Mário de Andrade emerged. The movement celebrated a Brazilian national identity that was rooted in transculturation, and Mário's *Macunaíma*, a novel, and Oswald's "Cannibalist Manifesto" were founding texts of the modernist movement.[1] Both texts insisted the only "authentic" Brazilian culture was a hybrid culture.

TRAVELING THEORIES AND AMERICAN DREAMS

These two components of Brazilian modernism—racial democracy and the defining of a Brazilian national identity as both syncretic and racially mixed—play out in African American literary and political discourse in the first half of the twentieth century. The representation of Brazil as a nation that privileges racial mixture and racial egalitarianism resonates in African American literature and mass communication produced during this period in the United States. In 1923, for example, Robert S. Abbott, editor of the *Chicago Defender*, visits Brazil for three months and returns to the United States touting Brazil's racial democracy and advocating black migration.[2] Mimicking Abbott's rhetoric, Brian Redfield, Nella Larsen's fictitious character in *Passing* (1929), identifies Brazil as a geography of freedom that would ensure the safety of his children and promise him full citizenship during a period of rampant lynching, segregation, and disenfranchisement in the United States. Ironically, the expression of Redfield's desire to escape to Brazil is never expressed through his own voice, but rather through his wife, Irene, when she repeatedly laments his silent desires: "That strange, and to her fantastic, notion of Brian's of going off to Brazil, which, though unmentioned, yet lived within him; how it frightened her, and—yes, angered her!" (187). Abbott and Larsen, however, do not address a critical tenet of Brazil's racial democracy propaganda—blackness as a disease that can be cured by "whitening" through miscegenation. And neither Larsen, Abbott, nor any of the other pro-Brazil black journalists and professionals who supported emigration to Brazil seemed to be aware that Brazil opposed black immigration on the grounds that it would "set back the whitening process" (Skidmore 196).[3] The Brazilian government did not publicize its bar on black immigration, as that would disrupt their promotion of a racial democracy.

By the 1960s, a UNESCO-sponsored research project conducted during the 1950s had revealed the myth of racial democracy in Brazil. The 1970s marked a period when the myth was openly contested by scholars and activists. *Corregidora* was published during this period in 1975, and *Caucasia* is set during this period but was published in 1998. These texts provide an interesting window for viewing how the idealized image of Brazil that emerged in the U.S. black press and literature during the 1920s made a critical shift in the post–civil rights era. In *Corregidora* and *Caucasia*, Brasilidade is revealed as a problematic ideology when appropriated in the United States. As a trans-hemispheric ideology, Brasilidade does not "absorb" blackness in the United States; instead, patriarchy is absorbed when the African American father is silenced and cut off from the African American family. In spite of my resistance to patriarchy and recognition of the gender inequalities it produces for women, silencing African American fathers and severing a black patronymic that has always already been contested in the United States is detrimental for both African American men and African American women. Anyone who champions the equal rights of African American women must also logically be concerned about the social and political status of African American men (but with no gender hierarchies that elevate one's status over the other). And in the case of these two texts, a decidedly feminist concern is paramount, because the silence produced by the Brazilianness rhetoric affects African American girls as well.

I am not the first scholar to interpret Gayl Jones's agenda in *Corregidora* as one invested in both African American women and African American men, but those interpretations often rely on the final pages of the text as the ultimate assurance that Jones's agenda is not invested in castration. Proposing that Martin is worthy of attention when considering a transnational context for this narrative is likely an unconventional proposition, but such a consideration promises fresh insight on ways that both a feminist and masculinist agenda might merge in black and diaspora studies. Martin is briefly Mama's husband only because he provided the sperm necessary for a Corregidora woman to "make generations." Like Mutt and Tadpole, Martin becomes a symbol of male violence and a source of traumatic memory for Ursa, especially when Mama recounts how Martin physically assaults her and shames her by forcing her to walk down the street holding up the ripped waistband of her pants as he exclaims, "'Go on down the street, lookin like a whore. I wont you to go on down the street, lookin like a whore'" (*Corregidora* 121). Ursa has not seen her father since she was two years old, and she has no memory of him other than what her mother shares with her after considerable cajoling.

Martin's absence is why he is critical to my analysis. Martin draws the most scholarly attention as the only man who has the courage to ask, "'How much was hate for Corregidora and how much was love'" (131). There is no excuse for Martin's physical abuse of Ursa's mother, but it is worthwhile to explore Martin's hatred for Ursa's mother and her grandmothers. Ursa's mother acknowledges that Ursa's grandmothers' monologues about Corregidora were not just prescribed for her ears but for Martin's too: "'They just go on like that, and then get in to talking about the importance of passing things like that down. I've heard that so much it's like I've learned it off by heart. But then with him there they figured they didn't have to tell me no more, but then what they didn't realize was they was telling Martin too . . .'" (128–29). Martin is forced to bear witness to a story that like Toni Morrison's *Beloved* is one "not to pass on"; yet, it is also a story that is so unbelievably cruel and demented that it lingers in the unconscious. This story presents an ugly twist to Brazil's racial democracy propaganda.

The Corregidora women embrace "the whitening thesis" and the white supremacist ideologies that fostered it. Their only self-perceived purpose in life is to bear witness to the atrocities of Brazilian slavery by making generations whose phenotype will bear witness to sexual assaults experienced by African-descended women. The rules that they follow when making generations have the peculiar essence of the Brazilian paradigm they love to hate: reproducing girls with light skin and lots of long hair (114, 117). The Corregidora women in the United States reproduce the hair, color, and bone hierarchies that Brazil believed would mask the hypocrisy of its racial democracy rhetoric. Outside of the Brazilian geography, however, these social theories are absent of any political praxis, and the democratic ideals that frame Brasilidade fall flat. Instead of producing a racial paradise, when transported to the United States these theories and praxis disrupt the African American family in ways that echo Daniel Patrick Moynihan's infamous and often criticized case study of the black family in 1965 in which, with urgency, he declared something must be done about the steadily growing number of households headed by African American women.[4] Moynihan warned that African Americans would be at a clear disadvantage in U.S. society if their families did not model the patriarchal structure of the dominant culture, which, according to his study, was already being evidenced through poverty, out-of-wedlock pregnancies, insufficient education, and crime. Appropriating the ideologies of Brazilianness in the United States, then, renders the African American father obsolete in *Corregidora*, because, as is witnessed with Martin, he is removed from the family after fulfilling his only duty of producing a whitened nation.

The relationship that Deck has with his family as a result of appropriating ideologies of Brasilidade in *Caucasia* is different from Martin's experience—Deck is not simply a sperm donor—but it is an experience that nonetheless silences him. *Corregidora* is a useful frame for my in-depth analysis of *Caucasia*. *Corregidora* privileges traditional tropes of African American women's writing: family, kinship and community; *Caucasia* does not privilege those tropes. The ways in which *Caucasia* parallels and diverges from *Corregidora* is indicative of critical differences between second-wave and third-wave black feminist agendas. Ursa's mother's reunification with Martin and Ursa's reunification with Mutt lack closure and raise critical questions about trauma and repetition.[5] Jones seems no more able to incorporate a community framed by a critical gender consciousness than can her fellow second-wavers like Toni Morrison, whose women brandish swords and pack guns at the end of *Paradise*. Perhaps what Jones and Morrison lack that Senna possesses is the ability to dream a different dream. Senna has the benefit of reaping the privileges of the trailblazing by second wavers, and inherent in that privilege is the freedom to *see* differently. Senna's sight is steeped in theory. *Caucasia* offers a theoretical framework for understanding the silenced father, the wistful daughter, and the fissured African American family that *Corregidora* only seems to be able to lament.

DISAPPEARING UTOPIAS AND SCIENTIFIC EXPERIMENTS

Birdie and Cole Lee are the daughters of civil rights activists. Sandy, their mother, is white and hails from a New England blue blood family. Deck is African American and a professor of anthropology at Boston University. When Deck and Sandy divorce, due to her white phenotype Birdie lives with her mother and Cole, due to her black phenotype, lives with her father. Shortly after the separation, Sandy becomes paranoid that she is wanted by the government for revolutionary activity and flees, first to a commune and then to New Hampshire, where she makes Birdie pass as Jewish. Deck also flees after the separation; he goes to Brazil with Cole and his girlfriend with the intent of writing a monograph about the greatness of Brazil's racial democracy. Birdie eventually runs away from her mother in order to find her father and sister and ends up in Berkeley, California.

Unlike Brian Redfield in *Passing*, Deck Lee pursues his fantasy of equality and freedom by actually traveling to Brazil. Although *Caucasia* does not dedicate any of the textual narrative to Deck's experiences in Brazil, it is clear from Deck's return to the United States that Brazil is not the racial paradise that either he or Brian were counting on it to be. Deck visits Brazil during the 1970s, after the myth of Brazil's racial democracy was becoming widely acknowledged. When Cole and Birdie reunite, Cole explains: "[O]ver those first few months in Rio, it had slowly dawned on them that the poor people living in the favellas resembled Africans, the rich people in power resembled Europeans, and everyone in the middle was obsessed with where they and their children would fall on the spectrum of color. Our father's disappointment over this realization had tainted everything; he was no longer able to see what was beautiful about Brazil" (*Caucasia* 346).

Ronnie, an old family movement friend, echoes Cole's understanding of Brazilianness when he explains Deck's enlightenment in Brazil to

Birdie: "Brazil was a bust. You know how he thought it was going to be this Xanadu, this grand Mulatto Nation? Well, he said he'd been wrong. It wasn't the racial paradise he thought it was going to be. There was some anthropological thing he had been looking for there. . . . But he said the Brazilians were more racist than the Americans" (303). Hanchard refers to Brazil as a "laboratory for racial egalitarianism" until the UNESCO report and others began debunking that myth (5); Deck experienced the debunking firsthand.

Brazil's absorption ideology mirrors what is ultimately Deck's own laboratory, his family. Because Deck is a professor of anthropology, it is fitting that he is invested in a scientific experiment of sorts that would debunk the racial science that anthropology was entrenched in at its inception as a discipline in the late nineteenth century. His marriage to his blue-blood, white wife, Sandy, and the children that they produce, Cole and Birdie, are not grounded in love and a desire for a family. Instead, Birdie notes that Deck "liked to joke to his friends that Cole and I were going to be proof that race mixing produced superior minds, the way a mutt is always more intelligent than a purebred dog" (22). Brazil is such a disappointment for Deck because the reality of the rubric of Brasilidade is that blackness is never completely absorbed, and thus, its racial democracy is revealed for what it truly is, a racist ideology that shares more in common with the United States than it does not.

The investment in Brasilidade and the scientific experiment that his family represents create a significant divide between Deck and Birdie. Deck's clear lack of interest in Birdie, his daughter whose white phenotype consistently marks her as not being his child, and his favor for Cole, his daughter whose black phenotype is more pronounced than his own, are obvious and hurtful for Birdie. Birdie notes, "I can't say that I enjoyed these visits with my father. He never had much to say to me. . . . Cole was my father's special one. . . . She was his prodigy—his young, gifted, and black" (47). Deck's lack of interest in Birdie almost becomes repulsion after an incident at the Public Gardens. Deck and Sandy have separated at this point, and it is a rare occasion when Birdie spends time with her father without Cole.

Although Deck does not have much to say to Birdie, which is typical, they do spend several hours walking around the gardens; they hold hands and go on a swan ride together, and Deck buys Birdie a T-shirt. All of these events lead Birdie to acknowledge to herself, "I felt closer to my father than I ever had before" (49). That closeness comes to an abrupt end when an older, white couple observes Deck and Birdie lying on the grass in the park. Unable to imagine the possibility of a "black" father having a "white" daughter, the couple informs two police officers of the "suspicious" black man with a white child. Even after Deck shows the officers a family picture and his faculty identification card for Boston University, the officers continue to grill him and Birdie, clearly insinuating their disbelief that he is her father and implying that he has abducted her. This event not only leaves Deck speechless—with nothing to say to Birdie—it also creates an irreconcilable distance between them. When Deck returns Birdie to her mother, Birdie laments, "Usually he kissed me on the top of my head before he said good-bye, but this time he just touched my forehead with the back of his hand, as if he were checking for a fever. His own hand was cold, and he pulled it away quickly, as if the touch had burned him" (52).

The incident at the Public Gardens discourages Deck from ever having any close and intimate time with Birdie again. Birdie reports, "He went back to ignoring me the way he always had" (61). And once Deck flees the United States to write his book in the Brazilian racial paradise, the "grand Mulatto Nation," he returns disheartened and with only one daughter. Birdie is dumbstruck by Ronnie's puzzled response that Deck has been back in the United States for several years when she inquires of his whereabouts in Brazil. Once Deck realizes that the disparities of the U.S. racial system are in fact an international phenomenon in spite of rhetoric that suggests otherwise, he abandons his "white" daughter, offering the lame excuse that, when he returned, "'I asked around, even tried calling some friends from Boston. But it was going to be difficult—a real project'" (332). Considering the difficulty of the "project" of locating his daughter, Deck opts for an alternative project.

RACIAL APHASIA AND PETRIFIED MONKEYS

Deck quite literally replaces Birdie with his seven-hundred-page manuscript, *The Petrified Monkey: Race, Blood, and the Origins of Hypocrisy*. He readily concedes that he has been consumed with writing his book, and, in fact, he expects that Birdie will be proud of his alternative project when he offers to let her peruse it. "He handed all seven hundred pages to me," Birdie explains, "smiling, as if it were a gift, as if I would be ecstatic to receive it" (333). The "origins of hypocrisy" that Deck's tome records is a reproduction of the history that was burned after slavery is abolished in Brazil, and it alludes to *Corregidora* in this way. The Corregidora women have the self-imposed duty of "making generations" in order to "bear witness" to the evil history that Brazil attempts to absolve when after emancipation the government burns all the documents pertaining to slavery. Ursa's grandmother explains, "'And then that's when the officials burned all the papers cause they wanted to play like what had happened before never did happen'" (79). The Corregidora women have the charge of bearing witness: ". . . *They burned all the documents, Ursa, but they didn't burn what they put in their minds. We got to burn out what they put in our minds, like you burn out a wound. Except we got to keep what we need to bear witness. That scar that's left to bear witness. We got to keep it as visible as our blood*" (72). Upon visiting Brazil, Deck realizes that the *visibility*—the evidence of racial mixture—that the Corregidora women strove for is a vexed and complicated set of politics in Brazil. The reality that Brazilian racial democracy encourages and depends on the erasure of blackness spurs Deck's obsession with revealing that hypocrisy in much the same way that the Corregidora women burdened themselves by reproducing visibly mixed-race daughters: the offspring must be female, because women reproduce nations.

Caucasia "is itself a signifying structure, a structure of intertextual revision, because it revises key tropes and rhetorical strategies received from precursory texts" (Gates, *Figures* 242), in this case, tropes of democracy and blackness not only in *Corregidora*, but also in *Passing* and the numerous editorials in African American newspapers during the 1920s that advocated emigration to Brazil. The title of Deck's book, *The Petrified Monkey*, demands that scholars consider the critical parody that Senna draws between the rubric of Brasilidade and the real, lived experiences of Deck, Cole, and Carmen, and more importantly, of Afro-Brazilian nationals. When placed in the Brazilian geography, the African American trickster figure, the Signifying Monkey, becomes the *Petrified Monkey*— a trickster figure who loses the ability to signify, who in effect loses all agency. To be "petrified" is to be paralyzed, or worse, deadened. The incorporation of blackness into the nation by absorption causes the Signifying Monkey to lose the ability to signify, to manipulate and transform language, and absorption ultimately strips him of his black subjectivity, and he becomes petrified.

In the context of both his book, *The Petrified Monkey*, and within the narrative of *Caucasia*, Deck is the Signifying Monkey. In order to silence the voice and paralyze the acts of the signifier (blackness) that "wreaks havoc upon the Signified [whiteness]" (Gates, *Figures* 238), the "whitening thesis" petrifies the signifier. If as scholar Henry Louis Gates Jr. notes, "signifying can also be employed to *reverse* or *undermine* pretense or even one's opinion about one's own status" (240), then this explanation offers insight into Deck's obsession with his book. Upon visiting Brazil, Deck realizes the reality of his status as a black person in Brazil, as well as his own complicity in his illusion. In an effort to validate the blackness that Brazil refuses to incorporate and in order to repair his own damaged psyche, Deck hopes that his book will *reverse* or *undermine* the pretense behind Brazil's racial democracy rhetoric.

The signifying that Deck performs is perhaps redemptive for him, but it fails to redeem his relationship with Birdie. The principle reason for that failure is that, even with new insight on the reality of race and caste in Brazil, Birdie remains nothing more than an experiment for Deck. And despite his denunciation of the utopianism he has invested in Brazil, Deck remains invested in the belief that U.S. racism can be eradicated in much the same way that Brazil asserted it could achieve a racial democracy—through racial mixing. His analogy between U.S. race relations and the status of the mulatto functioning as a canary in the coal mine reveals that he cannot break free from the idea that racial mixture can repair the nation. He presents his theory to Birdie, explaining how coal miners used canaries to determine how poisonous the air in mines was: "They would bring a canary in with them, and if it grew sick and died, they knew the air was bad and that eventually everyone else would be poisoned by the fumes. My father said that likewise, mulattos had historically been the gauge of how poisonous American race relations were. The fate of the mulatto in history and literature, he said, will manifest the symptoms that will eventually infect the rest of the nation" (*Caucasia* 335). Birdie and Cole are

Deck's canaries in the coal mine, even their names register their experimental relevance.

Like Brian Redfield, Deck laments that his skin, hair, and bone, regardless of how tinged they are with whiteness, will always already render him a second-class citizen, destined to reside on the margins of society and never be fully incorporated into the nation. His lamentation is compounded by gender. Despite playing the game right, not rocking the boat, attaining an education in the "master's" field (anthropology), Deck is and always must be an African American, something that Brian Redfield also learns when his medical practice and social status in the black community have no ability to elevate his status in the eyes of white America. Deck thought he could evade the duality of the African American identity in Brazil's racial paradise, but there too he was forced to face his blackness. The trans-hemispheric reality of blackness produces aphasia in Deck; his brain is literally injured by not only the reality of race throughout the Americas, but also by the degraded social and political status of Afro-Brazilians that is indicative of the failure of Brasilidade to absorb blackness. Deck's silence and distance from Birdie are a symptom of what I call *racial aphasia*.

Deck's racial ideologies and his obsessive pursuit to be incorporated into some nation, any nation, disallow him to be a parent in ways that parallel black family dynamics during slavery in the United States. His racial aphasia and his failure to parent are bound up in a legacy of slavery that stripped personhood from African American women and men, and in the process created a structure of misnaming. Hortense Spillers refers to this legacy as "American Grammar." Because Deck, like Brian Redfield and Martin, is denied a black patronymic within the black family structure, he turns to an alternative geography in hope of being able to claim "the name of the father" that the un-gendering power of slavery stripped from black men during slavery when they had no property rights and were, themselves, property. Having "been robbed of the parental right, the parental function," at the birth of his children, but especially during the interrogation at the Public Gardens, Deck forgoes paternity and instead tries to revise the codes that deny him a black patronymic (Spillers 78). The racial aphasia or ideological injury to the brain that Deck experiences spurs him to replace his daughter with a counter-narrative that reveals why he cannot claim the name of the father. The denial of a black patronymic and the production of a counter-narrative also, of course, respond to the "Moynihan Report" which notes the detrimental role slavery played in producing the social dilemmas of the black family in 1965.

Given Deck's newfound preoccupation with "setting the record straight," it is interesting that he produces two daughters; the Lee line ends with Deck, as both he and his sister, Dot, produce girls. Deck fails to father his daughters, and he literally fails to pass on the name of the father, a name that Deck learns is a grammatical error in the Americas.[6] As a result of there being no male heir to the multiracial nation in which Deck is invested, the multiracial woman becomes bearer of the nation. The burden that Deck places on Birdie and Cole, both as toxicity-detecting canaries and as biological reproducers, reflects the historic responsibility that women have held for either maintaining the purity of the nation, as is the case with white women, or contaminating the nation, as is the case with racially and ethnically marginalized women. Kate Chopin's short story "Desiree's Baby," for example, exemplifies how the United States imagines purity and contamination through a purely female paradigm.

The burden that women bear in relationship to the nation is reflected in the tenuous relationship that Deck has with Birdie. As the female line, Birdie, like Moynihan's indictment of African American women, is held responsible by Deck for his inability to hold "the Name and the Law of the father" (Spillers 66). Deck's experiment was to produce a mutt, not to produce whiteness, which is why he does not know what to do with Birdie and why he once points out an interracial couple to her as a *problem*— a eugenicist problem—evidenced in the woman's stringy hair and the man's ashy skin (*Caucasia* 62). In this sense, then, Birdie not only negates Deck's anthropological thesis, but as potential heir to Deck's multiracial nation, she also troubles notions of the efficacy of kinship. When speaking of Frederick Douglass's physical proximity to his siblings, yet his feeling of alienation from them after being separated from their mother, Hortense Spillers questions, "Can we say, then, that the *feeling* of kinship is *not* inevitable? That it describes a relationship that appears 'natural,' but must be 'cultivated' under actual material conditions?" (76).

MAMA'S BABY, PAPA'S MAYBE

The fact that Deck made no effort to "cultivate" a *"feeling* of kinship" is not the only aspect of his relationship with Birdie that reflects the limitations faced by families during slavery. Their relationship is strained because of his inability to pass on a patronymic to his white daughter, but it is also strained by the possibility that he did not father his "white" daughter. The character, Redbone, occupies a peculiar space in the narrative, particularly in relationship to Birdie, Sandy, and Deck. When Birdie first encounters Redbone, it is during a clandestine movement meeting. Redbone discovers Birdie peaking through a door, observing a room full of men and guns. When he is ordered to get rid of the little girl, his response is to squeeze Birdie's arm tight and respond to his commander, "Nigga, this ain't no ordinary little girl. This be Sandy Lee's little girl" (*Caucasia* 13). Redbone specifically identifies Sandy as Birdie's mother, but neglects to identify her as Deck's daughter. She is not Deck and Sandy Lee's daughter; she is simply Sandy's daughter, giving the power of maternity to a white woman and denying the African American man the power of paternity.

The question inherent in Redbone's selective naming is emphasized by Birdie acknowledging that, when Redbone picked her up to show her the guns, "I tried to squirm out of his arms. Something about the way he had said my name felt wrong. Too familiar." This problem with inappropriate familiarity is emphasized when Deck enters the room and is angered by seeing Redbone. It is important to note, however, that Deck does not articulate his anger as being about a problem with Redbone holding Birdie; instead, his anger is expressed as a distrust of Redbone's revolutionary authenticity. When Redbone explains that Birdie chose to eavesdrop and that she might not be so curious if Deck replaces his "high-falutin' theories" with guns. Deck responds to this insult that alludes to impotency by challenging Redbone's racial authenticity, a challenge that demonstrates no investment in actually protecting *his* daughter: "Don't tell me 'bout the revolution, you fake-ass half-breed motherfucker. . . . This ain't no brother. Where did this fool come from, anyway? Can someone tell me that? He shows up a month ago actin' like he been a revolutionary all his life. But no on knows where you come from, Red, do they?" The confrontation ends with Deck threatening, "If I ever see you near my wife again,

I swear man, it's all over" (14–15). The protective ownership that Deck extends to Sandy is not extended to Birdie—a wife is a sure "possession"; a daughter is, well, "papa's maybe."

Deck continues to be concerned about whether Redbone comes around Sandy, and by extension, his home, inviting Birdie to be his spy (49). The only concern expressed for Birdie's safety or well being is when Sandy learns that Redbone approached Birdie at school, talking to her and taking her picture through the fence. His conversation with Birdie alludes to her questionable paternity. When Birdie becomes uncomfortable with the exchange and announces that she must leave and return to her sister, pointing across the playground, Redbone replies, "Yeah. I see her. What happened there? You sure you got the same daddy?" Redbone follows that inquiry with an assertion that he and Birdie share common features. Birdie recounts, ". . . he watched me for a moment, fascinated by something on my face. I averted my eyes from his gaze. He said, 'You look like a little guinea. Anybody ever tell you that? That's what they used to say to me'" (93). In this instance, Redbone claims the name of the father, a claim whose validity is supported by Birdie's assertion that Cole's darker skin, nappier hair, and fuller lips are her father's "proof of the pudding, his milk-chocolate pudding." Cole's "existence told him he hadn't wandered quite so far and that his body still held the power to leave its mark" (47).

The notion of "leaving" his "mark" is an important one, because Deck's racial paradise differed from Brazil's in that he never wanted to absorb blackness. He instead wanted to produce a multiracial nation that would naturally absorb the construct of race. Deck, therefore, simply wants to dilute blackness, and in turn dilute whiteness as well, believing that the mutual dilution will create equality. Birdie's white phenotype—with no hint of blackness—spoils his experiment. Herein lies the problem with Redbone, too. Redbone is described by Birdie as looking "almost like a white man, barely a trace of black at all, except for his tight reddish-brown curls" (12). Thus, Redbone is the whitening theory in action. Provided he is Birdie's father as he alludes that he is, Redbone produces a phenotypically white daughter with Sandy, which is an additional reason why Deck is confounded by Birdie. Birdie is evidence of both his inability to ensure his own offspring and a foreshadowing of the disappointment that he will encounter in Brazil. Thus, it is convenient for Deck to suspect

Birdie's paternity, a suspicion that Birdie senses even without Redbone's insinuations: "Sometimes I wondered if it were my fault. I knew their marriage had begun to go sour at about the same time as my birth. They couldn't even agree on a name for me . . . [m]y birth certificate still reads, 'Baby Lee,' like the gravestone of some stillborn child" (17). The failure to name Birdie is significant for more than the birth certificate rendering her "like the gravestone of some stillborn child"—a life that never began; the failure to name also signifies on the black family in slavery, when parents could not take on the role of parents to name their children.

The question of paternity in *Caucasia* further compounds the nebulous naming of both father and daughter. In *Caucasia*, then, "'kinship' loses meaning" (Spillers 74). And it is through the negations and vicissitudes of familial relations that Senna breaks from an earlier black feminist tradition of privileging family and kinship. *Caucasia* challenges readers, and especially those engaged in black feminist discourse, to re-think bonds of kinship and family when she deconstructs the racial genealogies in which such bonds are rooted. Senna dreams a dream that is different from her literary precursors, Gayl Jones and Toni Morrison, and in her alternative way of *seeing* intersections between race, gender, and family dynamics, she offers a theory for understanding the challenges inherent in producing a critical gender consciousness. The gender rifts that Jones and Morrison leave in disrepair are produced and responded to differently in *Caucasia*. The reader is left with no hope that Birdie's and Deck's relationship can be repaired, because the racial democracy that Deck needs in order to claim the name of the father does not exist on either side of the equator. Just as Hurston and Hughes, Ursa and Mutt, and the Convent Women and Ruby are unable to reconcile their heterosexual gender differences, Deck and Birdie are left in silence.

In spite of the silence, Senna does propose a "solution," and it reveals the complicated reality of the social construction of race, particularly in the United States, where a social and legal history demands that its subjects are either white or black, but, until recently, never both or many. When discussing the conclusion of *Caucasia*, Lori Harrison-Kahan asserts, "Although *Caucasia* . . . privileges blackness over whiteness, the novel does not end with the act of 'loving blackness' alone. . . . Instead, *Caucasia* concludes with a validation of multiplicity" (43). So then, much like those she is apt to ridicule for celebrating a multiracial nation in her essay "The Mulatto Millennium," Senna also appears to believe in the political and social power of multiplicity, a concept that perhaps for her offers greater promise for allowing the father to speak and for the daughter to share his name. In fact, Birdie admits without shame that she does not want the historical and social baggage that comes along with blackness in the United States:

> Then I asked Dot, "What color am I? The last time I'd asked that question, I'd been in the woods of New Hampshire. Samantha had told me what color I was. She had said I was Jewish, but she had been joking, just playing along with what she knew to be a gag. Later she had told me I was black like her. At least that's what I had heard. Those words had made something clearer. *Made it clear that I didn't want to be black like Samantha. A doomed, tragic shade of black. I wanted to be black like somebody else.* (*Caucasia* 274, emphasis mine)

Birdie does not want to be black like Samantha, and she never suggests that she is or wants to be white like her mother. Birdie wants to be neither/nor, like the "dime a dozen" mixed-race children that Cole informs her attend Berkeley High. Like children on the school bus who in that shared space represent for Birdie a space where you are not bound by race—where blackness and whiteness are both absorbed and race no longer matters. This new nation, the *elemono* nation—the safe space, language, and people that Cole and Birdie imagined during childhood—differs from Brazil's purported racial democracy and proposes a solution to the disrepair at Jones's and Morrison's conclusions by replacing the familial kinship that is rooted in racial confraternity and genealogy with the kinship of the Multiracial Nation. The Multiracial Nation becomes the new family, bound by biological commonalities but not by shared DNA. Such a new family is particularly pertinent when one's biological family does not take ownership of its child/sibling.

The fact that neither Deck nor Cole attempted to find Birdie makes her urge to reconstruct family logical.[7] Even so, Birdie recognizes that the racial utopia that Berkeley High promises is not liberating for everyone: "I saw myself as a teenager in high school with a medley of mulatto children, canaries who had in fact survived the coal mine, singed and asthmatic, but still alive. Then I thought of Samantha and felt a wave of sadness. I wondered what would happen to her" (351). Birdie's sympathy toward Samantha's predicament as "tragically" black and not "cinnamon-spiced" like herself explains why, when Birdie reunites with her father at the conclusion of the novel, she is invested in claiming him as her father, never mentioning Redbone. Birdie ultimately embraces her father's canary-in-the-coal-mine theory, but differently. Birdie proposes that blackness is not pure and absolute as in the nationalist paradigms that frame earlier work by black women. She also does not privilege whiteness. *Caucasia* instead concludes with Birdie celebrating racial and cultural hybridity like the Brazilian modernists, but through a critical lens. The critical lens through which the celebrated hybridity of Brasilidade is viewed in *Caucasia* is a striking contrast to the uncritical ways in which the appropriation of Latinidad, Vodou, Candomblé, and the doctrine of the Nag Hamadi operate. The appropriation of Brasilidade in *Caucasia* is a particularly compelling critical appropriation because by interrogating the usefulness of such an appropriation through parallels— comparative race relations in the United States and Brazil—the racial experiences of African Americans in the United States becomes a transnational one that does not rely on travel.

CHAPTER 5

The Sight/Site of Transgression in *Eve's Bayou*

The past is not dead; it is not even past.
—William Faulkner

My spirit comes here to drink.
My spirit comes here to drink.
Blood is the undercurrent.
—Joy Harjo, "New Orleans"

Such endings that are not over is what haunting is about.
—Avery F. Gordon, *Ghostly Matters: Haunting and the Sociological Imagination*

Although there are worthwhile gains to be made through critical appropriations, those performed in *Louisiana* and *Paradise* also demonstrate the dangers inherent in the act of appropriation—Ella dies and the Convent women must be on constant guard. The collaborative work between Beyoncé and Shakira, as well as Beyoncé's appropriations of Latinidad on her *B'Day* CD demonstrate that even a critical gender consciousness does not erase potential pitfalls in appropriating the cultural theories of another culture or ethnic group. *Caucasia*, however, approaches the construction of an immobile transnational identity by actually interrogating the types of ideologies that Brodber and Morrison privilege in their texts. In a similar fashion, Kasi Lemmons resists privileging appropriations of diasporic cultural theories at the same time that theories of hybridity frame her film. By delving into what it means for an African American family to construct a home space in a Louisiana bayou in 1962, Lemmons explores how racial wounds produced in racialized geographies haunt the present, making it difficult to sustain healthy family and social relationships.

Lemmons uses the trope of incest as a means to emphasize the cultural and racial hybridity inherent in the United States, while also warning viewers of the stasis that can be produced as a result of immobility. Incest acts as a signifier of U.S. imperialism, revealing the transnational matters that are unique to people who dwell in a nation within a nation, which is a type of transnational subjectivity. By setting the film in Louisiana and utilizing the trope of incest to frame the narrative, Lemmons signifies heavily on the historical memory that is inscribed within that geography, particularly when she signifies on William Faulkner's *Go Down, Moses*. If viewers consider incest in this film as a signifier of the racial residue inherent in Faulkner's text, instead of focusing on the apparently titillating possibility of molestation that many critics and viewers are enraptured by in the film, then incest becomes no more than parody. Kasi Lemmons's film, *Eve's Bayou*, appropriates theories of hybridity in order to create a counter-narrative about both African American women and African American men's experiences with race, gender, memory, and geography in the United States. Her emphasis on the collective, black transnational experience—women *and* men—and localizing those experiences in a specific U.S. geography provide an exciting look at new directions in African American women's cultural productions. The critical appropriations in Lemmons's work function differently from those in the previous chapters. Lemmons insinuates that African Americans already embody transnational identities by virtue of the cultural contact zones produced by slavery. Instead of claiming diasporic theories of cultural identity from elsewhere in the diaspora, Lemmons demonstrates how theories and the reality of cultural and racial hybridity were a naturally occurring process in the United States, too—a naturally occurring process she encourages viewers to visualize.

Lemmons's attention to immobile transnational identity formation is through the use of tropes of incest and hybridity, which facilitate visualizing transnational African American cultural identities and various other libratory ways of seeing. Seeing new images of African Americans and the African American family in *Eve's Bayou* and understanding their significance is critical to registering the more radical, figurative incest Lemmons invokes through geography and memory. Ultimately, to borrow from bell hooks, Lemmons "invites the audience to look differently"

(*Black Looks* 130). The new images are part of Lemmons's larger project of correcting a U.S. patriarchal and cultural memory that makes stereotypical and essentialist notions of African American identity acceptable and, in all too many cases, celebratory. Lemmons troubles how viewers see—how viewers see race as diverse U.S. citizens, how viewers see the past, especially its ramifications on the present, and finally, how viewers might see differently.

Eve's Bayou is set in 1962 in an unnamed Louisiana parish, probably a commutable distance north of New Orleans. The film has been categorized as a coming-of-age story, southern gothic, and a black family film. The opening shot of a man and woman having sex against a wall in the dark and its reflection through a child's eye does not fully prepare the viewer for the woman's voice over that declares, "The summer I killed my father, I was ten years old." The remainder of the opening voice-over explains the Batiste family's lineage. The now grown Eve Batiste explains that her great-grandmother, also named Eve, cured her slave master, General Jean-Paul Batiste, of cholera. In return for saving his life, General Batiste freed Eve, giving her Eve's Bayou. Eve goes on to add facetiously, "Perhaps in gratitude she bore him sixteen children."

The film is structured around the lives of Louis Batiste (Samuel L. Jackson), a physician and philanderer; his wife, Roselyn (Roz) Batiste (Lynn Whitfield), who is disappointed in her marriage yet remains the exemplary 1960s wife; and their children, Eve (Jurnee Smollett), Cisely (Meagan Good), and Poe (Jake Smollett). Louis's sister, Mozelle (Debbie Morgan), also occupies a central role in the plot and in the Batiste family. As a psychic counselor, sometimes voodoo practitioner, and a "black widow" who has buried three spouses, one as a result of her own infidelity, Mozelle is a complicated foil to Louis. They are both perceived by their community to be healers—Louis steeped in conventional Western medicine and Mozelle committed to a syncretic mix of Old and New World cures.

The event in the film that critics and scholars have devoted the most attention to is Cisely's revelation to Eve that their intoxicated father molested her one stormy evening. Being acutely aware of her father's philandering and fearing the threat that it poses to her family, Eve seeks out the local voodoo priestess, Elzora (Diahann Carroll), paying her twenty dollars to kill her father. Louis ultimately "falls on his own sword," as

Elzora insinuates might happen to him, without the work of voodoo. The husband of a woman with whom he had been having an open affair shoots him outside a bar. After her father's death, Eve finds a letter he had written to Mozelle expressing his concern that Cisely had attempted to seduce him, attributing her behavior to adolescent confusion. When confronted by Eve, Cisely admits that she really does not know what happened on that stormy evening. The two sisters embrace and cry together as Eve forgives Cisely, and they both forgive their father for having been unable to give them everything they need. The film ends as they submerge the letter in the bayou, and Eve's voice-over repeats the opening lines of the film, this time omitting the reference to killing her father and instead expressing the complicated nature of memory and its relationship to the past: "We are the daughters of Eve and Jean-Paul Batiste. I was named for her. Like others before me, I have the gift of sight, but the truth changes color, depending on the light, and tomorrow can be clearer than yesterday. Memory is a selection of images, some elusive, others printed indelibly on the brain. Each image is like a thread, each thread woven together to make a tapestry of intricate texture. And the tapestry tells a story, and the story is our past."

A FORETHOUGHT ON AUDIENCE

I missed *Eve's Bayou* at the box office. Its debut in 1997 was at the end of an era of black film that I often found disappointing and producing little intellectual stimulation.[1] A number of years after its debut, when a friend insisted that I needed to watch *Eve's Bayou,* I was pleasantly surprised. The black middle-class focus of the film has become familiar in both twenty-first-century mainstream and independent black films, but representations of the black middle class in black film during the 1990s was something of an anomaly.[2] Even television was limited in its depiction of the black middle class, with only *The Cosby Show* airing in the mid-1980s through the early 1990s and *The Fresh Prince of Bel-Air* originally airing in 1990 through the mid-1990s.[3] In addition to the dearth of films that attended to the black middle class and black life and culture in nonessentialist ways, with the exception of Julie Dash's *Daughters of the Dust,* which I viewed in an undergraduate English seminar, I had never viewed a film written and/or directed by an African American woman. However, although Forrest Whitaker and Kevin Rodney Sullivan directed *Waiting to Exhale* and *How Stella Got Her Groove Back* respectively, Terry McMillan did participate in the writing of the screenplays. The film adaptation of *Waiting to Exhale*—what bell hooks has called "mock feminism"—and *How Stella Got Her Groove Back*—what Wyclef Jean has referred to as U.S. black women's sexual tourism—did not provide me with any more intellectual stimulation about the complexities and diversity of African American life and culture than did the highly popular gangster films that flooded theaters in the 1990s.

My dismissal of McMillan's film adaptations and of the popular gangster and "hood-life" films of the 1990s should not be understood as the critique of someone who never views a film purely for entertainment. Because black film, like so much of black cultural productions, often has the twofold intention of entertaining and making social commentary, I believe it is fair to expect more than entertainment from them. Thus, I approach black film in particular with a critical, and often cynical, eye. In "The Oppositional Gaze: Black Female Spectators," bell hooks refers to my movie-viewing cynicism as an "oppositional gaze"—a way of viewing that black women spectators have developed as a form of resistance that allots them agency—the power to resist, disrupt, and re-invent—as doubly marginalized viewers in a racist and sexist culture. hooks argues that some black female spectators find that "looking too deep," or consciously identifying "with films . . . made moviegoing less than pleasurable; at times it caused pain" (*Black Looks* 121). During the 1990s, my oppositional gaze urged me to take a break from black film and resulted in missing *Eve's Bayou* in the theaters. Despite being hailed the film of the year by many critics, Kasi Lemmons's independent film was not the box office hit that McMillan's mainstream films were. Furthermore, when I consult with my black female friends about their reaction to the film, those who have seen it describe it as good, not because of the hope it projects that they can "have it all," like McMillan's films, but because it is, well, so odd. I attribute the paradoxical relationship between "good" and "odd" to be an issue of *sight*.

Film and cultural scholar Jacqueline Bobo notes, "[w]hether we, as filmmakers or as critics, agree with the sentiments expressed by members of the audience, it is important to consider their reactions within the totality of their lives" (Black Popular Culture 70). Bobo's emphasis on audience is directly related to her experience interviewing black women about their reactions to the film adaptation of Alice Walker's novel The Color Purple. Bobo concludes, "It is a mistake to value the comments of the critics at the expense of a more wide-ranging examination of the ways in which audiences make sense of cultural products . . . the ideal is a thinking audience" (73). My use of Bobo's assertion is not to suggest that viewers who experienced visual pleasure from mainstream 1990s film do not think, but rather that different audiences view differently. The same friends who thought Eve's Bayou was "odd" felt that the McMillan adaptations were "real" representations of what African American women's lives were really like. This difference speaks to the beauty of Lemmons's narrative and directorial prowess. Lemmons employs creativity and skillful intellect when she offers oppositional spectators a gaze that resists, transgresses, and "create[s] alternative texts that are not solely reactions" in order to challenge essentialist notions of blackness (hooks, Black Looks 128).

Just as many African American female spectators made sense of the McMillan films (and gangster films) in ways that I resist, many of my students who are unfamiliar with the historical social conditions the majority of African Americans experienced during the 1960s marvel at the Batiste family's wealth and accomplishment. The film is set in 1962, which is the same year James Meredith integrated the University of Mississippi, only two years after the sit-in movements begin, and only one year before the March on Washington, the assassination of Medger Evers, and the infamous Alabama church bombing. When I teach this film, many white students breathe a sigh of relief when they realize that this unfamiliar film is not yet another indictment of white denial of African Americans' full rights of citizenship. Many African American students feel a sense of hope seeing a seemingly unmolested, affluent African American family going about its life during the middle of the civil rights movement. The film gives both African American and white students what I am confident is an unintended assurance that we are a nation no longer stratified by Du Bois's color line, if in fact it ever existed.[4] My students' responses to Eve's Bayou are not isolated. The tenderness of their youth does not fuel their naïveté. I say this because numerous film critics, life-seasoned men and women, also insist on viewing *Eve's Bayou* as a race-neutral film that engages "universal" issues like infidelity, dysfunctional families, sibling rivalry, youthful innocence, Oedipal complexes, and murder.

The various "universal" transgressions that this film encapsulates, particularly the "incest scene," act as distractions from a much more significant transgression that Lemmons is attempting. *Eve's Bayou* emerges at a time in black-directed film history when strategies of black visual representation, as well as criticism of black films, began undergoing dramatic transformations. Valerie Smith explains that the shift was marked by a shift away from the "positive/negative" debate, and toward films that worked to offer "alternative, truer representations of black life" than those presented, say, in D. W. Griffith's *Birth of a Nation* (1). Stuart Hall refers to this shift as one preoccupied more with the diversity of the black experience rather than with its homogeneity (Valerie Smith 4).[5] Lemmons recognizes the shift when she explains that "I would like to see movies where the black female characters act like real women, the women that I know, the women in this room—our mothers, our sisters, our friends. A well-portrayed, well-rounded female character with depth" (Hardy). The wish that Lemmons expresses is transgressive in the sense that it defies the popular perceptions and representations of African American women that are projected globally by the U.S. media. Her wish is reminiscent of the kind of transgressive acts Zora Neal Hurston performed when "Hurston was determined to write about black life as it existed apart from racism, injustice, Jim Crow—where black people laughed, celebrated, loved, sorrowed, struggled—unconcerned about white people and completely unaware of being 'a problem'" (Washington, Intro, *I Love Myself* 17).

As a film that is attuned to issues of diverse representation, *Eve's Bayou* baffled many film reviewers and general viewers alike, as evidenced by the discussions questioning whether it is in fact a "black film" and the urge to de-racialize the film as "universal."[6] The category and universality debates suggest that many viewers have no knowledge base with which to understand and decipher the new images of black culture and the transgressions that Lemmons presents. It also means, as Mia Mask asserts, viewers are stuck on "the hegemony of whiteness as the locus of universal humanism." This belief leads Mask to point out, "Just because *Eve's Bayou*

provides a picture of the Creole bourgeoisie doesn't mean these people—
or this film—cease to represent an African-American experience. Most
reviewers remain unaware of how fully entrenched most colored folks are
in middle-American values and are therefore more likely to praise such
films than critique them for a dependence on generic conventions" (27).

Mask's point echoes Lemmons's acknowledgment that she wanted
"deep Southern glamour" in the film, because it was a reality of her childhood (Alexander 259). Because most viewers are entrenched in the ever-
prevailing visual economy of race, most viewers cannot imagine that such
a black family existed in 1962. They also cannot imagine transgression
beyond the literal, distorting their view and ultimately obscuring any productive understanding of transgression in the film. It becomes impossible to imagine sexual transgressions like adultery and incest that reflect anything more than phallocentric dominance and Oedipal desire.[7]
Such a lack of imagination unquestionably guides the minimal scholarship devoted to a film that was the highest-grossing independent film at
the U.S. box office in 1997. Moreover, with few exceptions, when *Eve's
Bayou* does receive scholarly attention, the analysis consistently attends to
interpreting the incest and adultery transgressions as bound up in patriarchal constructs of power and desire.[8] Some scholars are also compelled
to cast their "did it–didn't do it" verdict (as are many viewers, especially
my students).

I find this discussion of fault to be just as unproductive as the strong
urge to debate *who* the "white girl" is in Toni Morrison's *Paradise*. Both
debates overlook the more complex narratives operating in the text by allowing the audience to avoid engaging critical questions. In other words,
debating and being distracted by which of the women is white diminishes
the atrocity committed when the men burst through an unlocked door and
massacre unarmed women. The audience, then, is asking who is the white
girl rather than how can something this heinous occur in a society that
claims to be civilized. Similarly, the attention to casting a guilt/innocence
verdict in *Eve's Bayou* distracts from the intricacy of a narrative that calls
upon viewers to think about how race, gender, memory, and place can
produce unique narratives. By debating guilt or innocence, the audience
risks failing to ask the critical question of why audiences and critics have
rather easily assigned and accepted Louis's guilt.

The obsession with transgressions coupled with the desire for a race-neutral universality prevents viewers and scholars from recognizing the much grander transgressions that Lemmons engages in. Lemmons asks audiences and scholars to imagine one particular history that can be remembered productively in the present, but ceases to haunt those struggling to live in that present. Lemmons's construction of characters and representations of figurative incest work concomitantly with the critical appropriation of hybridity. The relationship between character construction and figurative incest pushes the audience to "see" African Americans differently—differently from 1990s black film depictions as well as differently from mainstream media depictions. Ultimately, *Eve's Bayou* resists being positioned in a purely nationalist context and instead emphasizes a transnational context that focuses on the cultural hybridity of African Americans. Such a focus explains why the civil rights movement is not foregrounded, though the threat of danger and violence is alluded to indirectly, and instead the cultural hybridity that positions Louisiana as part of the extended Caribbean is highlighted.

SUPERWOMEN AND BLACK MACHO

Lemmons develops and attends to her female and male characters equally; both the black female and the black male experience are bound up in the historical memory that permeates the southern geography. The images that she creates of these women and men, however, are complex. "This Disease Called Strength: Some Observations on the Compensating Construction of Black Female Character," an essay by Trudier Harris, and "Black Male Trouble: The Challenges of Rethinking Masculine Difference," by Michael Awkward, provide insight into why what might seem like simple character constructions are indeed complicated. Harris calls on scholars to reconsider how both black male and black female writers' depiction of black female characters as strong, unbreakable, and unfeeling beings can in fact be destructive—can be a disease that dominates both black females' lives and the lives of their loved ones. She argues that as "towers of strength" black women characters often become "malignant growths upon the lives of their relatives" (109–10). Because strength was once the only virtue granted to black women, Harris notes that it became a dominant trope in black fiction.[9] Despite the agency and subjectivity the "tower of strength" image bestows upon real and imagined black women, Harris insists that it is time for this image to be deconstructed because its continued presence is at "the detriment of other possibilities and potentially stymied future directions for the representation of black women" (110).

Harris performs an insightful close reading of both black male and black female–authored fiction from 1942 to 1992. She completes her analysis of the disparate texts by noting that such "superhuman" depictions deny black women characters access to a self that experiences leisure, breakdowns, and failures that are prerequisite for them to be seen as "complex, feeling human beings" (122). What I hear echoed throughout Harris's essay is an encouragement, if not demand, for black writers to develop more expansive and imaginative forms with which to depict black women characters. While I appreciate Harris's contention that black fiction needs more diverse images of black female characters, I do not advocate the erasure of "towers of strength" images from black fiction. Such erasure operates as a subtle persecution of black women who are dubbed "strong," whether they seek the title or not.

Eve's Bayou presents black female characters that "defy spatial and bodily limitations, commune with the dead, or die and continue to be sentient" (Harris, "This Disease Called Strength," 121), while they simultaneously disrupt the "superwoman" myth. They disrupt the myth through their awareness of their humanness—through their self-recognition of failures, weaknesses, and strengths. By presenting feeling, well-rounded black female characters, like Roz and Mozelle, who recognize the multiplicity of these qualities within themselves, Lemmons offers a way for black female characters to "be strong" without it becoming a disease that debilitates them or those they love. Mozelle and Roz Batiste possess strengths, weaknesses, and failures; they are not the strong black women who induce illness in those around them or in themselves.

This becomes particularly apparent if contrasted against the Batiste matriarch, Eve Batiste. The younger Eve explains in the opening voiceover: "The town we lived in was named after a slave. It's said, that when General Jean Paul Batiste was stricken with cholera, his life was saved by the powerful medicine of an African slave woman called Eve. In return for his life, he freed her and gave her this piece of land by the bayou. Perhaps in gratitude, she bore him sixteen children. We are the descendants of Eve and Jean Paul Batiste. I was named after her." I do not think the younger Eve is proposing that her great-grandmother had a power and agency that made her "strong," but the description provided does fit the characteristics that are often used to describe black women as strong, neglecting to consider just how little ability they had to truly act for themselves and be their own agents. The fact that the younger Eve offers this ancestral history upfront suggests its importance to our understanding of the contemporary Batiste family.

TENDERNESS IS A DEEPER THING THAN CRUELTY

Roz Batiste tries to be an attentive wife and mother. She follows all the tenets of bourgeois culture. She dresses impeccably, her hair is coiffed and nails are manicured, all while preparing meals, hosting parties, and raising three children under a classical Western rubric. In spite of the cultural values that she embraces, Roz recognizes that she does not "have it all."[10] The black female characters that Harris critiques typically struggle against significant economic limitations that contribute to their "disease." Although Roz clearly enjoys a bourgeois lifestyle in which money is the least of her concerns, she recognizes the failures in her marriage. After learning of yet another of Louis's shameless affairs, Roz explains to Mozelle that Louis has always known "how to fix things": "I always wanted to be a doctor's wife. When I first met Louis, I watched him set a boy's leg that had fallen out of a tree. And I thought, here's a man that can fix things. He'll take care of me. He's a healer. Louis swore that by the time he was thirty, he'd be a famous specialist. And doctors from around the world would come to him for advice. And I believed him. Because it seemed like he knew everything. So I leave my family and move to this swamp, and I find out he's just a man" (42).[11]

Roz reveals that she never viewed Louis as a partner; she viewed him as a caretaker, a healer. Her view of Louis demonstrates that financial gain and economic security do not enable the racially oppressed to transcend race. Such monetary gains do not facilitate the repair of racial wounds. As a refined black woman, devoted wife, and dutiful mother, Roz works to repair the wounds caused by popular and persistent negative images of black womanhood.[12] Roz recognizes that, due to her desire or need to be "fixed," she imposed superhuman powers on her husband that he could never possess—superhuman powers similar to those that black-authored literature has imposed on black women.[13]

In addition to experiencing weaknesses and failures, Roz approaches mothering with a style that differs from the "tough-love" style that Harris reports so many pre-1992 black female characters directed toward their children in order that they themselves might be prepared for and survive in a racist society. Roz locks her children in the house in the middle of a Louisiana summer because of Elzora's ambiguous warning, "look to your children," and because of Mozelle's vision of a child being hit by a train. This decision seems irrational to both Louis and the children; nonetheless, the efforts by Roz to protect her children are markedly different from the physical and/or verbal abuse and even murder that Harris describes. Even when Cisely repeatedly challenges her mother, Roz only once responds with force. After Cisely openly defies her mother's house arrest by walking to town to visit her father, catching the bus to the beauty salon, and crossing the train tracks when walking back home, Roz slaps her impulsively. Cisely responds to the slap by giving her mother a defiant glare and walking away triumphantly as her mother stands in the doorway looking ready to crumple. Later that evening, Roz explains her actions to Cisely, offering her the explanation and assurance of love that Harris argues was absent in earlier texts: "When I was your age, I was just like you. I thought I knew everything. Now, even the things I'm most familiar with seem mysterious to me. But I know *I love you*. And it's my job to protect you, as best I can. If you disobey my orders and leave this house again, I swear, I'll lock you in your room" (Lemmons 77).

Although Roz performs an isolated act of violence toward Cisely, the act is followed by Roz's efforts to explain her actions and verbally assure her daughter that she loves her. This scene is one of several that allude to dangers—perhaps racial dangers—outside of Eve's Bayou. This scene also presents a stark contrast to mothers like Mrs. Macteer in Toni Morrison's *The Bluest Eye* or Elizabeth Grimes in James Baldwin's *Go Tell It on the Mountain*, mothers who can show their children no softness with which to counter the "tough love." Lemmons creates a character in Roz whose strength does not overshadow her tenderness, softness, or the "complexity of [her] femininity and humanity" that Harris argues happens all too often with other black female characters ("This Disease Called Strength" 114). Roz's tenderness, softness, and the complexity of her humanity linger with viewers when, after Louis's funeral, Roz, Cisely, Eve, and Poe are all in their mother's bed. Her arms embrace each of them as she experiences the happiness and unimagined "end" to her problems that Elzora insisted she "look to [her] children for."

Mozelle Batiste complicates matters because she is not a mother. The women Harris focuses on are all mothers; however, despite her childlessness, Mozelle is "motherly." In fact, her motherliness presents an interesting contrast to Roz. Mozelle and Eve both have the "gift of sight" and have a particularly strong relationship with one another. As the middle child, Eve often feels forlorn and rejected. In the opening scene, during her parents' party, Eve shows clear resentment that her father dances with Cisely in front of their guests, while she only belatedly receives the promise, "From now on, we'll dance at every party. . . ." Feelings of resentment are also apparent when Eve taunts Poe, her mother's "baby." While Poe is mama's baby and Cisely is daddy's darling, Eve, the precocious tomboy, consistently seems out of place. Mozelle steps in to provide Eve with motherly care and attention, to become the quintessential southern "two mama." But there are some things about Mozelle's mothering that are rather untraditional. Both Mozelle and Eve possess clairvoyance and other-worldliness that allows them to see what others cannot see. This shared "gift of sight" draws them together instinctually in a manner different from a mother-child manner. Mozelle shares the sordid details of the deaths of her three husbands with Eve. Eve is Mozelle's comforter after the death of Harry, Mozelle's third husband. Eve arrives at Mozelle's house the day after the funeral to ensure that Mozelle gets out of bed and is prepared for her clients. She combs her aunt's hair and tries to convince her that she does not "look so bad." It is as if Eve, the ignored middle child, can on a certain level relate to the unprecedented losses Mozelle experiences through the death of her husbands, an understanding that is assumedly driven by her "gift of sight."

In contrast to the tender relationship that is guided by Eve's and Mozelle's kindred spirits, there is another side that is marked by threats of violence. Mozelle never physically assaults Eve in the film, but she often threatens to harm Eve, as well as others. Mozelle is quick to threaten, "I will kill you" or "I will do you harm." It perhaps is not surprising then that Eve, the ten-year-old protégé of Mozelle, makes her own death threats, the most significant one being when Eve seeks out Elzora to do voodoo on her father and kill him in retaliation for the pain she believes he caused Cisely. This shared tendency to threaten physical violence toward others presents an interesting contrast to Louis's non-physical acts of violence toward his family through his extramarital affairs.

SIGNIFYING ON A DREAM DEFERRED

When read together with "This Disease," Michael Awkward's essay "Black Male Trouble: The Challenges of Rethinking Masculine Differences" offers a counterpoint for understanding how Lemmons deconstructs both "superwomen" and macho men in *Eve's Bayou*. Awkward begins with a review of mainstream feminist and black feminist entanglement with essentialist and antiessentialist representations of women's relationship to masculinity. In what he admits to be an encapsulated form, he offers a history of the tensions between black feminism and mainstream feminism during the 1970s (294) and insists on the elimination of any prevailing conceptions of monolithic masculinity.[14] Awkward's essay provides a complementary reading to Harris's essay because, if writers are to invent new black female characters, it would also make sense that new black male characters must exist as their counterparts. Without this double invention, the new female characters would be doomed to revert to inevitable past traditions. Thus, in a brief analysis of *Eve's Bayou*, Awkward argues that Louis's character cannot be interpreted simply as a philandering, self-centered husband and father. Louis must be understood, Awkward insists, as "an extremely sympathetic portrait of black masculinity" (297); we cannot simply view him as a man who "abuses his masculine power" (302). Awkward argues against such a view because he posits the film as less a cautionary tale about the dangers of patriarchy and more about the troubling relationship between memory and history.

Louis Batiste is the dominant male character in *Eve's Bayou*, and in the minimal critical scholarship on this film he receives most of the attention. This attention has merit; Louis is the leading man, and Samuel L. Jackson, the most familiar actor in the film for most viewers, plays his character. Awkward's "Black Male Trouble" offers a thoughtful feminist analysis of Louis's character and actions, and D. Soyini Madison offers a compelling psychoanalytic interpretation in "Oedipus Rex at *Eve's Bayou* or the Little Black Girl Who Left Sigmund Freud in the Swamp."[15] Considering this attention, I will instead focus on Julian Grayraven, a black male character who defies the monolithic constructions of black masculinity that Awkward critiques, as well as one who offers an important opportunity to examine black female characters who respond to Harris's call for reinvention.

Julian Grayraven arrives on Mozelle's front porch seeking a reading. He says he is far from home, though he does not reveal where home is. As he explains that he has spent the last year searching for his wayward wife, he admits that he has "no home to return to anymore." There are two important points to be made about the construction of Julian's character. First, he is not indigenous to Eve's Bayou. He arrives from some unknown place; yet, he makes himself at home once he arrives in the bayou. The second point is that Julian represents a racial and cultural hybridity that is inherent in the Batiste family, but that Lemmons takes care to emphasize more so with Julian. The Batiste surname is French, but one could easily surmise it is a slave master's name without knowing the family history. Grayraven, Julian's surname, is a Native American surname that he likely would only have inherited through blood. Reflecting that surname, his character has long, straight hair, high cheekbones, and darker skin, all of which suggest an Indigenous-African mixture. The way that Julian is able to interpret Mozelle's marital maladies also are suggestive of what is often perceived to be an indigenous sort of epistemology.

> MOZELLE: Bad things happen to people that marry me. . . . All my husbands die. And I like you too much to kill you.
>
> GRAYRAVEN: Then I will die from loving you. It's inevitable.
>
> MOZELLE: Julian, I'm serious. I think I'm cursed.
>
> GRAYRAVEN: I will break the curse.
>
> MOZELLE: I can't have children. I'm barren.
>
> GRAYRAVEN: You're not barren, you're wounded . . . here . . . (he touches

her heart) from loving too much . . . and from losing those you love. It's here that I will plant seeds.

The seeds that Julian plants are steeped in a radical redefinition of terms. In his mind "barren" does not mean lacking, devoid, or incapable; it means wounded, which means that barrenness can be eradicated by being receptive to something different. Julian's promise and interpretation are particularly provocative if we read Mozelle's barrenness figuratively as a lacking produced by racial wounds and the losses that are produced by those wounds, rather than the inability to reproduce offspring.

Julian plants the seeds of life. In the case of the Batiste family, life is synonymous with forgiveness and redemption, which is directly connected to the issue of incest in the film. The opening narration and cinematography of Eve's Bayou suggest that, as William Faulkner said, "the past is not even past." The narrator makes the jarring declaration that she killed her father during the summer of her tenth year, as well as presents a history of Eve's Bayou that is bound up in property, rape, and miscegenation. Such revelations acknowledge the same sense of death and haunting implicit in Joy Harjo's perception of New Orleans being a city steeped in blood and in Avery Gordon's proclamation about the interminableness of the past and its relationship to the present, a view that echoes Faulkner's claim. Furthermore, the draping Spanish moss, the murky bayou water, and the expansive sugarcane fields invoke an eeriness or uncanny effect that resonates with the narration. These three intersecting references help to articulate the melancholic effects of slavery on those living in the present. Such historical residue makes it virtually impossible to identify discreet boundaries between the past and the present.

Lemmons signifies on a white-written text's haunting presence in the black imagination. By signifying on William Faulkner's Go Down, Moses, Lemmons troubles the inclination of audiences and scholars to read incest in this film literally. My purpose in discussing Go Down, Moses is to identify and analyze a significant intertextuality between Faulkner's text and Lemmons's film. My primary interest is in Faulkner's chapter "The Bear," a hunting story that is circumscribed by the geographies of race. It analyzes racialization as what geographers Audrey Kobayashi and Linda Peake refer to as "part of the normal, and normalized, landscape" (392) of the United States through issues of land ownership and environmental stewardship, the vanishing wilderness, the pervasiveness of white privilege, and the always troubling union of miscegenation and incest.

Isaac "Ike" McCaslin is shamed by the connections between his family history and the destruction of land, as well as the rape and incest that was performed in order to maintain power and ownership of the land. He is particularly appalled when he discovers in his uncles' old ledger books that his grandfather, Carothers McCaslin, fathered his daughter with his slave, Eunice, and later fathered his granddaughter with the child he fathered with Eunice.[16] Eunice kills herself as a result of the complex emotions arising out of this family history. As a result of Ike's shame, he repudiates his grandfather's monetary legacy and rejects his birthright to the land, deferring it to his cousin, McCaslin Edmonds. Ike chooses not to reproduce biologically and to refuse the law of primogeniture—a type of reproduction—in an effort to eradicate his family's sins against nature and humanity. It is important to note, however, that the McCaslin incest would not have been viewed as transgressive, as would the Batiste incest. Slave women were property and had no bodily rights. Ike views his grandfather's acts as transgressions because he views slaves as possessing an identity beyond that of property. Although the situation surrounding the incest differs in *Go Down, Moses* and *Eve's Bayou*, the repetition is marked by a racialized U.S. geography that never ceases to haunt the present—what sociologist Avery Gordon refers to as "[s]uch endings that are not over" (139).

I want to rethink sexual transgression in this film, as well as the noted absence of a white presence in the film. While Ike's discovery of family incest is Faulkner's representation of what Toni Morrison calls "the ghost in the machine" —"for the ways in which the presence of Afro-Americans has shaped the choices, the language, the structure—the meaning of so much American literature" ("Unspeakable Things Unspoken" 11)—incest in the Batiste family does the opposite through its demand that the pervasive, undying presence of whiteness be acknowledged as a destructive force in this family, even in its seeming absence.[17] The alterations that Lemmons makes to her black female and black male characters allows for an interpretation of the sexual transgressions, particularly the incest, in a way that transcends patriarchal and hegemonic readings. Incest in

Eve's Bayou can be understood as a signifier that calls up the racialized geography inherent in Faulkner's work, and that inevitably repeats itself in Lemmons's film.

Lemmons signifies by playing on the so-called universality of "family matters" that elicited favorable approval from film critics. She also plays on the idea that incest is a universal social transgression, an unquestionably taboo act of love that all cultures reject. I am not suggesting that Lemmons, like Faulkner, is proposing that incest and love are synonymous. I am arguing that, like the slave narratives, Lemmons makes "the white written text speak with a black voice, [which] is the initial mode of inscription of the metaphor of the double-voiced" (Gates, *Signifying Monkey* 131). In other words, the trope of incest in *Eve's Bayou* functions as the "double-voiced" text that talks back to *Go Down, Moses*. My assertion here is that, as employed by Lemmons, incest is no more than parody in *Eve's Bayou*. Her "use of repetition and reversal (chiasmus) constitutes an implicit parody of a subject's own complicity in illusion" (Gates, *Figures* 240). When viewers and film critics understand *Eve's Bayou* to be a universal, de-raced film, they are demonstrating their own limitations in interpreting meaning—they essentially are like the Lion in the narrative "Signifying Monkey" poem: "the Signifying Monkey is able to signify upon the Lion only because the Lion does not understand the nature of the monkey's discourse[. . . .] The monkey speaks figuratively, in a symbolic code; the lion interprets or reads literally and suffers the consequences of his folly, which is a reversal of his status as King of the Jungle" (241). This is one of many reasons why it is problematic to say that this is a film that "anybody can relate to."

It is not fair to simply fault viewers and scholars for not understanding the nature of Lemmons's discourse. Without being placed in a cultural and historical context, the incest scenes are rather ambiguous and difficult to "read." The first version of the scene is presented from Cisely's perspective when she reveals to Eve why she needs to get away from their father. The same evening that Cisely defies her mother and leaves the house, Roz informs Cisely that she will wait up for Louis, ending what had become a nightly ritual for Cisely. It is a stormy evening, and when Louis returns home in the middle of the night, the argument that ensues is so loud that Cisely and Eve are awakened by their parents' voices. Louis and Roz are arguing about Cisely's behavior and Roz's knowledge that Matty Meraux, a "loose" woman, has been hanging around Louis's office. When the arguing has concluded, Cisely disobeys her mother and goes downstairs to comfort her father; she fears that her mother's "nagging" might cause him to "divorce" the family. Louis is sitting in a chair, half passed out. Cisely approaches him from behind and begins massaging his shoulders, telling him she came to make him feel better. He takes one of her hands and guides her to the front of the chair to sit on his lap. She kisses him lightly on the lips in an appropriate manner. Then Louis leans forward and kisses her in a manner that is entirely inappropriate. Cisely pushes him away with her arms and knees, which causes him to relent and smack her, knocking her to the floor.

Louis's version of the events of that evening is much different. It is presented posthumously through a letter that he assumedly intended to give Mozelle. He was prompted to write the letter as a result of Mozelle accusing him of molesting Cisely. Eve discovers the letter and is infuriated with her sister, because Louis's letter makes Eve feel betrayed by her sister. Louis describes the first kiss as "the sweetest kiss a daughter could give a drunk and guilt-ridden father—a kiss of redemption." Then, he says Cisely kissed him like a woman. In his startled state, he slaps her to the floor and she runs off. Louis wishes that he could have the moment back so that he could hold her and comfort her and discuss the situation with her—putting the boundaries back in place.

I have suggested that audiences' and scholars' heightened attention to these scenes is problematic because it obscures a more significant transgression. But first it is critical to read these two scenes, which ultimately necessitates that I, too, cast a verdict. Cisely's version of the event simply reinforces concerns viewers ought to already have picked up on. Cisely displays a classic Electra complex.[18] She waits up for her father every evening and fixes him cocktails. She is envious when Eve receives his attention. She cuts her hair like her mother and accuses Roz of not being a proper wife to Louis. This behavior, as well as the stormy night scene, culminates in the arrival of Cisely's menstrual cycle. As a variation of the Electra complex, Cisely begins to develop her mother's character type with the hope of keeping her father from divorcing his family, rather than with the hope of attracting a man similar to her father. When Louis slaps

Cisely, she is jolted from her senselessness in the same manner that she hopes her sweet "kiss of redemption" will jolt her father from his philandering ways. The fact that so many audiences and scholars overlook the Electra complex and are comfortable with reading Louis as a child molester is indicative of a society that readily accepts the representation of black men as hypersexual beings.[19] The popular and historical hypersexualization of black men makes it easy for viewers and scholars to accept without interrogation that Louis is so sexually deviant that he would even molest his own daughter. However, if these two scenes are *not* interpreted as the most significant site of incest in this film, viewers will be able to appreciate a much more fruitful way of understanding incest in a racialized geography.

If incest is not indeed incest in *Eve's Bayou*, then what is it? The possible incest committed either by Louis or by Cisely, depending on interpretation, signifies upon African Americans' "transgressive" desire for incorporation into the U.S. body politic—to be viewed and treated as full-fledged citizens. Incest is used figuratively to represent the desire of African Americans to be seen differently—not to be seen as immutable prototypes, but as complex, feeling human beings who desire a singular identity. This complex subjectivity spurs Claudia Tate to argue, "[i]f we persist in reductively defining black subjectivity as political agency, we will continue to overlook the force of desire . . . in the lives of African Americans" (*Psychoanalysis* 10). *Eve's Bayou* depicts no overt signs of political agency; yet, "the force of desire" in the lives of the Batiste family remains overlooked. Critics and scholars have ignored the motif of the American Dream in this film, and particularly how such dreaming is inescapably shaped and controlled by race. The Batiste family has seemingly achieved the American Dream. This is the very reason why the civil rights movement is not engaged. Viewers who know history know it is occurring, but the point is that by not engaging the movement and the violence that spurred it, attention or emphasis is placed upon "the force of desire" that compels the Batiste family to pursue the American dream. Lemmons's act of omission is not an oversight but rather a transgression against the U.S. politics at that time that resisted allotting full citizenship to African Americans. Upon casual observation, the Batiste family fits squarely and comfortably into southern bourgeois society. A deeper look, however, reveals that there is so much residue—rape, incest, miscegenation—from a slave past that haunts the family in the present. Such hauntings effectively prevent full access to the American Dream. The hauntings in this film speak to contemporary discourse surrounding notions and efforts to be post-race. The hauntings demand that we acknowledge the difficulty of transcending race in a nation whose very being still depends upon racial stratifications.

DE RAILROAD BRIDGE'S A SAD SONG IN DE AIR

Eve's Bayou is set in a location that lacks a physical "white" presence and is geographically isolated.[20] The entire film is set in Eve's Bayou. Other than Mr. Meraux's professorship at Xavier University in New Orleans, Roz's brief lament that she gave up everything to move to the swamp with Louis, and Cisely's departure to live with her maternal grandmother, we have no sense that there is a world outside of Eve's Bayou. The townspeople appear to be unharmed and unmolested by the turbulence of the civil rights movement. There are no televisions or radios that connect their lives to the politics or culture of the outside world. Eve's Bayou is an exceptionally insular, isolated community. Insularity focuses the viewers' attention on the interiority of the characters' lives, and it helps viewers to accept the psychological bent through which they can fully appreciate the transgressions.

This insularity ought to have raised the question of incest well before the "stormy night" scene in which viewers are left wondering who kissed whom. By "incest" here, I mean incest literally as an actual sexual transgression. For example, Elzora, the voodoo practitioner Eve asks to curse her father, explains to Eve that Louis's wax coffin is buried "Down there where all them/Batistes is buried." This explanation coupled with Elzora's insistence that Mozelle is a curse, a black widow, on a surface level point to death, but can also be linked to familial incest. The Batiste family started out as a large family. Eve Batiste birthed sixteen children. In just three generations that large family seems to have vanished just like the families in Ruby dwindled over generations. Louis and Mozelle are the only children mentioned from their line, and Mozelle has no children. Her husbands keep dying as if a supernatural force is ensuring that she remain barren in an effort to obliterate the incest. In such a small, insular town, there is never any mention of extended family. Furthermore, when Roz locks the children in the house after Mozelle's vision, Louis remarks that she has been in and out of mental institutions, suggesting a mental defect that could be linked to a pattern of incest. Considering the insularity and the seemingly unprecedented number of dead Batistes, it is plausible that the disease in the Batiste family is not "tower of strength" African American women, but rather an unhealthy desire for one's self. While the film does not provide enough evidence to argue that the incest is the "royal incest" that the McCaslins employ to maintain power, or the incest that Ruby perpetuates to maintain racial "purity," the film does offer enough context to understand it as a peculiar predicament of the Batiste family that precedes the "stormy night." Thus, the physical incest in this film is not bound up in two ambiguous scenes; the physical incest is staying home or the refusal to move out of the home space, and the body of the mother/sister/daughter, much like Ruby's unwritten law against "scattering" in *Paradise*.

Eve's Bayou is isolated, but the railroad is a potential outlet to the outside world, and it helps illuminate the connection between death and incest in the film. It is also significant for understanding the legacy of both familial and figurative incest. Railroads embody a dual symbolism.[21] They are emblems of modernity at the same time that they are markers of technological and cultural imperialism. In *Dixie Limited: Railroads, Culture, and the Southern Renaissance,* Joseph R. Millichamp points out that, on the one hand, for writers of Faulkner's generation, "The newly important rail network represented the reconciliation, prosperity, and sophistication necessary for a Southern literary flowering . . ." (12). On the other hand, however, "African American writers from the days of the Underground Railroad through the Great Migration of the twentieth century saw the trains of the South as ambivalently situated symbols of both escape and entrapment" (20). Trains inevitably carried a mark of death for African Americans because the tracks were often laid with disproportionate African American male convict labor.

Trains appear in two significant scenes in the film. The first scene is immediately after Mozelle has her fortune told by Elzora, when Elzora hisses, "I don't need chicken bones to tell your fortune, Mozelle Batiste.

You're a curse. A black widder. Next man that marries you is a dead man. Like the others. Always be that way" (Lemmons 45). Upon leaving the market area, Mozelle collapses after seeing a vision of what appears to be and sounds like a train rushing toward her and Roz. Based on this vision and Elzora's insistence that Roz "look to her children" for comfort, Roz is sure that one of her children will be struck by a train if she does not keep them within the perceivably safe confines of their house. A bus, not a train, does eventually hit a child, and the Batiste children are freed from house arrest.[22]

The second train scene occurs when Lenny Meraux confronts Louis and Matty in King's Bar at the end of the film. Lenny is seen walking alongside the train tracks in a dark overcoat and a fedora that obscures his face. His gait is slightly askew, yet his determined stride reflects his intent purpose. His approach is marked by the distant sound of a train. As he continues to approach the bar, confronts Louis, and attempts to leave with Matty, the sound of the train becomes louder and louder. Finally, when Lenny shoots Louis, the train passes by them, drowning out other sounds and eventually obscuring our view.

The railroad becomes a significant connector between incest and death. The movement of the train and the progress that it indicates create a striking contrast against Eve's Bayou the town, as well as the people. Lemmons signifies on "The Bear," as the railroad in that text and in her film is a violation of the pristine and a challenge to static perfection. Eve's Bayou is stagnant. Few people come, and few people leave. The stagnation is reminiscent of the stagnation in Ruby, with the difference being that Ruby more successfully closed itself off from outsiders. The recurring presence of the train in Eve's Bayou serves as a constant reminder of the impossibility of transcending the borders of the present. The trains, like Cisely's accusation of molestation, disrupt the Batiste family's sense of perfection and security, revealing a diseased past.

Railroads can also be phallocentric symbols that represent patriarchal power. Louis is educated and accomplished; he has a family, property, and a certain degree of power in the community. Yet, according to D. Soyini Madison, he needs to be a "hero," he needs to be desired. Scholars are correct when they analyze the character of Louis as one that subscribes to patriarchal and hegemonic ideals. Such an analysis, however, does not attend to the sense of loss that Louis so desperately strives to retrieve. The Spanish moss and voodoo-enchanted forests do not cause the uncanny feeling that this film induces; the uncanny feeling is produced by the overwhelming racial geography of the setting. Louis attempts to transcend the racialized geography of his home space by trying to become Roz's healer and other women's hero—by being what Mark Anthony Neal refers to as a "Strong Black Man."[23] By doing so, he fails to attend to the present, particularly his family. Louis, like the 8-rock in *Paradise*, has failed to understand that "utopia is not a place that you can go; we are always only in the here and now" (Kawash 6). Louis is so consumed with trying to escape the burdens of the past and be "strong" in the present that his efforts manifest into acts of transgression against his family. The most significant way in which he transgresses is in his failure to be the father and husband that his wife and children need, because he is too preoccupied with needing to be a hero. This preoccupation with heroism and failure to attend to his family make it possible for his family to believe he is capable of harming his daughter.

Although Louis fails as a husband and father, he should not be viewed through a purely negative lens. The past racial wounds that haunt the present drive his transgression. His need to be a hero is bound up in a past that emasculated African American men. Despite the inescapable history, Louis's death can be viewed as a redemptive act. It provides the opportunity for his family to locate a safe home space in the present. This is most evident in his communication with Mozelle through a dream in which he grants her the *grace*—something the Convent women also sought in *Paradise*—she has searched for so desperately in each of her marriages. Mozelle has a dream in which she is flying, and she sees a woman drowning from the corner of her eye. She realizes that she is the drowning woman. As she is contemplating whether she should save her, Louis's voice interrupts and says "don't look back." Mozelle continues to fly and lets her other self drown. She wakes from the dream having decided to marry Julian.

In "Imagining Race and Religion in Louisiana," Carolyn M. Jones suggests that Louis's character has an additional redeeming quality. When Louis pushes Eve out of the way of Lenny's gunfire, Jones argues, he performs a "redemptive repetition of his pushing, whether in anger or surprise, of Cecily [*sic*]" (113). Louis's death, or his "fall on his own sword," eradicates the Batiste family of the physical and figurative burden of incest that haunts the family. Louis's death alone, however, cannot perform this eradication completely, and neither can the "kiss of redemption" that he says Cisely bestowed upon him on the "stormy night." While Louis's presence in the film is marked by death and incest, Julian's presence is marked by life.

A SUNDAY KIND OF LOVE

Kasi Lemmons "invites her audience to look differently" (hooks, *Black Looks*, 130). The alternative view that she proposes gives the audience the choice, or at least the opportunity, to think about African American life and culture more critically. The two different perspectives of what "really happened" on that stormy night and Cisely's belated admittance that she does not know what "really happened" is not just about an alternative way of understanding the past, but is also about an alternative way of *seeing* the past. It is similar to Consolata Sosa's discovery in *Paradise* that it is "a question of language." For Consolata, "seeing in" is a gift that is steeped "in sight." This possibility that "in sight" can enable characters to suspend judgment in the face of ambiguous situations provides insight into a new image of black maleness that Julian represents.

The ambiguous ending of *Eve's Bayou* certainly does not cast Louis Batiste in the most favorable light. The infidelity and eventual absence of Louis, however, opens a space in the Batiste family for a new social organization. This organization relieves men like Louis from the need to be heroes, while also relieving women from feeling obliged to be "towers of strength." This new social organization, one that is neither patriarchal nor matriarchal, is steeped in partnership rather than kinship, and it is guided by human fallibility rather than superhuman strength. Julian promises to plant seeds in Mozelle's heart. While this can be viewed as a patriarchal and phallocentric expression, it is nonetheless significant in the context of the Batiste family and its relationship to the past. Julian is able to "see in" and, as Morrison's Beloved says, "touch [Mozelle] on the inside." Julian represents an alternative to the black macho that is Louis's nemesis. Because Julian knows himself and is not invested in gender constructs, he is able to *see* what Mozelle and her family need. Julian is particularly successful at constructing a space in which he and Mozelle can embrace a partnership in which both partners can experience a life grounded in work and pleasure, not having to give up one in order to accomplish the other, as did Ella in *Louisiana* and Zora Neale Hurston in real life.

The opening and closing voice-over suggests that, like Mozelle, Eve is also receptive to being touched on the inside. "I have the gift of sight, but the truth changes color, depending on the light, and tomorrow can be clearer than yesterday. Memory is a selection of images, some elusive, others printed indelibly on the brain." The film begins with a voice-over that admits, "The summer I killed my father . . . ," but the closing voice-over begins, "The summer my father said goodnight." The difference reinforces Eve's insistence that "truth changes color." In this instance the "truth" acts as an agent of reconciliation—it allows the past to be reconsidered through a different lens. Eve, like her aunt, learns how to remember the past in a way that allows her to become free from the past. Like the lesson Eve learns, the film itself seems to want to teach its audience a lesson as well.

The characters are not the only ones who learn lessons, for *Eve's Bayou* also instructs its audience. To return to the paradox of African American female spectators, there is a lesson for them as well, because their sight is connected intricately to the sites of transgression in this film. As educated middle-class or soon-to-be middle-class black women, my friends needed to celebrate black women's experiences on the screen, regardless of how pathetic they might be, as a way of legitimizing their own raced and gendered experiences. What bell hooks, Jacqueline Bobo, and I have observed about many black female spectators is that they want the "Sunday kind of love" that Etta James croons out while Julian paints a portrait of Mozelle. If they hold out hope for that kind of love that "lasts past Saturday night" and one that takes them off of the "lonely road that leads to nowhere," then they just might have it all. Like *Caucasia*, then, *Eve's Bayou* concludes with a radical re-conception of the relationship between African American women and transnationalism. Similarly to the hip-hop songstress Beyoncé Knowles, who insists that she can construct her own hybrid identity, Senna and Lemmons embrace hybrid black subjects and culture, but unlike Knowles, they are more rigorous when they interrogate the implications and consequences of appropriating diasporic cultural identities. *Caucasia* and *Eve's Bayou* demonstrate that the appropriations do not make the art and people transnational; the art and the people are always already transnational by virtue of the location and nature of their production. And, perhaps, this is Lemmons's message to her black viewers, especially black women: to move out of the familiar home space—the body of the mother—and to begin looking differently at how they view themselves.

Loose Your Mother

A Different Route Home

M oving outside of familiar home spaces—the body of the mother— could produce the possibility for radically re-conceptualizing the racialized self in the United States. The texts I have analyzed suggest that a paradigm centered on racialized kinship and community not only pigeonholes African Americans into a localized and homogenous space, but that such a paradigm can also prove detrimental, as is demonstrated in *Paradise* and *Louisiana* when the lives of African American women become casualties of nation building. Shifting the paradigm in a way that privileges heterogeneity and searches for and is accepting of home spaces that do not assume sameness creates the possibility for imagining alternative notions of kinship and community that enable African Americans to develop more complex sensibilities about nation and belonging, as well as to embrace transnational identities that make them feel more at home in diaspora.

Lose your mother. This simple sentence that Saidiya Hartman uses to title her memoir chronicling her experiences in Ghana and along the Atlantic slave route is open to multiple translations. As Hartman employs it, the sentence describes the orphaning of diaspora blacks that lost their kin and country as a result of the transatlantic slave trade. This meaning, in fact, is the catalyst for Hartman's sojourn in Ghana and her journey along the slave route; she hopes to be homed: "To lose your mother was to be denied your kin, country, and identity. To lose your mother was to forget your past" (85). Spurred by a Du Boisian double consciousness and a pervasive sense of unbelonging, Hartman hopes to locate a home space, roots, origins, kin, safety, belonging in what, on the one hand, many African Americans call the motherland. On the other hand, as many other African Americans already suspect, Hartman learns that "home" is an

elusive term that is full of meaning at the same time that it can be mean-
ingless for African Americans. Hartman quickly learns that, not only are
there no kin looking for her or missing her in Ghana, but that the stranger
she perceives herself to be in the United States is an identity she also embodies in Ghana. She must reluctantly admit, "Contrary to popular belief, Africans did not sell their brothers and sisters into slavery. They sold
strangers: those outside the web of kin and clan relationships, nonmem-
bers of the polity, foreigners and barbarians at the outskirts of their country, and lawbreakers expelled from society" (5). Her journey to "excavate a
wound" perhaps offers her some sense of closure at the end, but it fails to
enable her to no longer "feel like a problem." In this case, when one loses
one's mother, the mother cannot be retrieved—"she becomes a myth."

Lose your mother. Hartman's use of this sentence as a metaphor for
her journey implies that the mother has been lost. The sentence could,
however, also be understood as an imperative, a command to lose one's
mother, to give up the ghost of an irretrievable past and a lost love object
that cannot be reincorporated into the self. She encounters few Ghana-
ian sympathizers; most find her presence and her Swahili name amus-
ing, if not irritating. While the Ghanaians she perceives to be distant kin
could be issuing this command—lose your mother—the command certainly was issued from the slave traders who bought Hartman's kin and
transported them to the Americas. Lose your mother.

Loose your mother. Loose. Lose. Both words are quite similar phoneti-
cally and in spelling, yet different in definition. Can loosing the mother,
as one would loose or cast out a ghost or demon, allow the orphan to
imagine an alternative home and a different kind of kin? This is a question that Hartman inevitably has to ponder, "But when does one decide
to stop looking to the past and instead conceive of a new order? When is
it time to dream of another country or to embrace other strangers as al-
lies or to make an opening, an overture, where there is none?" (100). The
questions Hartman poses make me wonder whether her experience in
Ghana and even her motivation for going would have changed if African
American identity formation was more often thought about as a unique
process of transculturation—a process when as a result of a variety of different cultural contacts, some things are lost, new things are gained, and
the result is a new hybrid identity. Thinking of African American identity

formation in this way not only makes the "contact zone" home, but it also recognizes the value and relevance that transnational sensibilities can bestow upon African Americans, particularly those who are immobile, staying put in the United States. The concept of an immobile transnationalism that homes African Americans registers how "sometimes folk need more," as Lone DuPres plainly states in *Paradise*. Sometimes folk need more than patriarchal and nationalist notions of community, family, and kinship can provide—an understanding of racialized relationships that failed Hartman, Consolata, and Ella.

The idea that people of African descent throughout the world share a common sameness due to their African ancestry proved to be dangerous for Consolata Sosa in Toni Morrison's *Paradise*. The cultural similarities that drew her to the Ruby townspeople and ultimately led to an affair with Deacon Morgan by no means meant that Consolata and the Ruby townspeople were indeed the same ideologically. Their differences were undeniably apparent when a band of men from Ruby orchestrated a massacre based upon their beliefs that the Convent women were unnatural, had "powers," and did not need God or men (God and men ultimately become synonymous in Ruby, Oklahoma). While the narrative makes it clear that the blame placed upon the Convent women is no more than Ruby projecting its own downfalls onto them, it becomes obvious in *Paradise* that a shared blackness does not mean a shared sameness.

Although there is no physical conflict in *Louisiana*, the text provides an opportunity to further examine the relationship between gender, kinship, and community and the role romantic notions of diaspora plays in that relationship. The nationalist paradigm that is privileged in *Louisiana* through négritude and Pan-Africanism constructs New Orleans as a utopian space where African-descended people can celebrate sameness, failing to register the problematic gender politics of such communities relying on sustenance from one woman. Beyoncé's politics around performance and production are indicative of an effort to reject narrow proscriptions of family and community. A transnational sisterhood produces a complex blackness that positions African American women like herself at the center of transnational discourse. While *Caucasia* is a hard-nosed critique of uncritical appropriations of diasporic theories of cultural identity, both *Caucasia* and *Eve's Bayou* insinuate that not only can African Americans develop transnational identities without moving across national boundaries, but that the realities of the transnational flow of culture and the Americas as a contact zone often impose transnational identities on those who might not be consciously pursuing such identities. The focus on kinship, family, and community in the latter two texts emphasizes the need to rethink these tropes in black women's studies, to consider whether the tropes have remained the same, and to ponder whether new tropes are emerging.

The pressing need to be more imaginative regarding ideas of kinship, family, and community is also demonstrated through the frequency that incest appears in African American women's cultural productions. While I directly engage metaphorical incest in *Paradise* and *Eve's Bayou*, arguably, incest haunts all of the texts I examine. In using the term "incest," I am thinking metaphorically about incest as incorporation. In other words, the critical appropriations that are performed in each text are efforts to incorporate into the self particular ways of knowing that produce a new, transnational identity. The new self is comfortable moving outside of the body of the mother and exploring other communities. The new self realizes that kinship must be cultivated and is not naturally produced due to similar phenotype. The new self troubles both traditional discourse in African American and diaspora studies and transnational studies. African American and diaspora studies continue to struggle with a critical gender consciousness, and diaspora studies consistently defines diaspora subjects as those who migrate, moving across national borders. African American studies in particular privileges a nationalist paradigm that understands blackness to mean a shared sameness of culture, values, and ideologies. And transnational studies neglects to consider seriously the idea that the development of transnational identities within the confines of national borders contributes to a more nuanced understanding of transnationalism and identity formation.

The questions Hartman concluded with directly intersect with the conclusions I have drawn about the texts I examined and their engagement with transnationalism. Must home always be elsewhere? What can be gained from looking outside of the mother for kinship and community? The answers that have emerged in my analyses would suggest that there are benefits in imagining and embracing the idea that home is right here, not elsewhere. The idea of home being here in the United States fosters a claim to citizenship and belonging that often eludes African Americans who cannot imagine home being here. I propose that one way for African Americans to feel at home in diaspora is through the appropriation of diasporic theories of cultural identity. The act of appropriation could home some African Americans who need "more" at the same time that it disturbs the narrowness of transnational studies.

NOTES

159

INTRODUCTION

1. I am alternating between "black" and "African American" here to distinguish between racialization and ethnicity. The artists I examine are all racialized as black, though not all of the artists are U.S.-born. The texts I examine, however, focus primarily on U.S.-born or African American women regardless of the ethnicity of the artist producing the text.

2. For a detailed analysis and bibliography of how considerations of transnational or trans-hemispheric studies add more nuanced dimensions to the literary and cultural studies of the Americas (including the United States), see Caroline F. Levander and Robert S. Levine's "Introduction: Hemispheric American Literary History."

3. Schomburg was a noted bibliophile, curator, and historian. His exceptional collection of materials on the life and culture of people of African descent is housed at the Schomburg Center for Research in Black Culture.

4. Mary Helen Washington, "'Disturbing the Peace: What Happens to American Studies If You Put African American Studies at the Center?' Presidential Address to the American Studies Association," 29 October 1997.

5. I resist the temptation to trace "truth telling" back to Phillis Wheatley, whose work in many ways positions her as a literary foremother of African American transnationalism. As a captured Senegalese slave, Wheatley embodies the more accepted understanding of transnationalism that is centered on crossing national borders. Thus, her experience as a transnational subject falls outside of my point that a paradigm shift is needed so that *transnational* and *travel* are not inherently linked concepts, which is why I identify slave narratives—texts and a genre indigenous to the United States, at least initially—as the earliest example of African American women's "truth telling."

6. See Elizabeth McHenry, *Forgotten Readers*.

7. Barbara Smith, *The Truth That Never Hurts*, 3–21.

8. I use both "African American" and "black" as descriptive adjectives, but I am not using them interchangeably. I use "African American" to be specific about women of African descent who are not only U.S. citizens, but who also are descended from U.S. slaves. I use "black" much more broadly to identify all people of African descent in the United States. The usage is important in this study because many of the key figures in establishing and

continuing black women's studies have roots elsewhere, particularly the Caribbean; yet, they may not be identified as African American.

9. While Davis has traveled and lived outside the country and Shakur has political asylum in Cuba, both women's political ideologies have traveled globally, regardless of whether they have ever been to those places.

10. In *At Home in Diaspora: Black International Writing,* Walters uses a theoretical framework opposite to the one I employ. Walters examines black writers who are writing from outside of the nation they call "home." Nonetheless, conceptually, our sense of the need to "be at home" in a home that is not home-like is similar, and thus, I find the phrase useful for articulating the political agenda at play in the texts I examine.

11. I am signifying here on George Schuyler's (1931) satirical novel of the same title that critiqued the preposterousness of race as a social construct.

12. In "Punks, Bulldaggers, and Welfare Queens: The Radical Potential of Queer Politics," Cathy J. Cohen raises a similar point through her discussion of transformational political work.

13. See George Shepperson's "African Diaspora: Concept and Context" as a classic essay that engages the etymology of *diaspora* and its use in black studies.

14. There are many terms circulating that attend to the movement and displacement resulting from modernity. They can often seem synonymous and often are in fact used interchangeably. *Cosmopolitanism* is one such term. It is often used interchangeably with *transnational.* While there is no one agreed-upon definition of cosmopolitanism, scholars seem to consistently identify a global humanism as the very essence of cosmopolitanism. It is perhaps the global ethics that define the debates around cosmopolitanism that make it fall outside the scope of this project. The texts I examine do not interrogate the nation and national identity formations because of an investment in universal humanism and global citizenship. The texts are not presenting a treatise on how to coexist in a human community. This critical difference, then, is why the concept of cosmopolitanism is not particularly useful for this project, in spite of the conceptual parallels between cosmopolitanism and the ways in which I engage concepts of diaspora and transnationality.

15. See Thomas LeClair, "The Language Must Not Sweat: A Conversation with Toni Morrison."

16. Wendy W. Walters, *At Home in Diaspora: Black International Writing.*

17. Brent Hayes Edwards. *The Practice of Diaspora: Literature, Translation, and the Rise of Black Internationalism.*

18. Darlene Clark Hine documents the relationship between gender and travel through a historical lens in *Hine Sight: Black Women and the Re-Construction of American History.* Carol Boyce Davies examines the gendered nature of travel through a diasporic lens in *Black Women, Writing, and Identity: Migrations of the Subject.* For analysis of the relationship between travel, space, and agency in African American women's writing, see Mary Helen Washington's introduction to Harriet Jacobs's "Incidents" in *Invented Lives: Narratives of Black Women, 1860–1960,* Claudia Tate's *Black Women Writers at Work,* and Deborah McDowell's essay, "New Directions for Black Feminist Criticism."

19. Joanne M. Braxton and Andrée Nicola McLaughlin coined this expression in their edited collection *Wild Women in the Whirlwind: Afra-American Culture and the Contemporary Literary Renaissance.*

20. Paul Gilroy is one of the most noted proponents of what he positions as "post-race" discourse in the humanities. In earlier work, but especially in *Against Race: Imagining Political Culture Beyond the Color Line,* Gilroy argues for a "radical nonracial humanism" instead of antiracist discourse. He insists that scholars reify race when they consistently acknowledge it as a social construction, but then continue to use the terminology. In the social sciences, William Julius Wilson is perhaps the most recognized proponent of post-race discourse. In *The Declining Significance of Race: Blacks and Changing American Institutions* (1978) Wilson argues that the significance of race is waning and that class difference is the greater determinant in social equality.

21. In "Literatures of the Americas, *Latinidad,* and the Re-formation of Multi-Ethnic Literatures," Katherine Sugg explains, "The January 2003 *PMLA* issue on 'America, The Idea, The Literature,' is an emphatic example of the former perspective, in which various critics posit transnational perspectives as more politically engaged and nationalist ones as conservative, or even regressive" (229).

CHAPTER ONE

1. While there is a shared concern between how Walters employs this phrase and the way I do in this chapter, our use of the phrase is notably different. We both are concerned with the sense of unbelonging and homelessness so frequently expressed through black cultural productions throughout the African diaspora. Walters, however, understands "being at home in diaspora" to be produced through the political act of writing in exile. My use of the phrase focuses on black subjects who have stayed put, black people who are trying to negotiate the geopolitics of race from countries that they do in fact call home—they want to be at home in diaspora rather than leaving or imagining home as an unrecoverable land of origin.

2. The manifesto was originally published in Portuguese in the first issue of *Revista de Antropofagia* as "Manifesto Antropofago."

3. Originally published in French as "Éloge de la créolité."

4. Some scholars have noted the presence of some of these unidentified beings I identify as visitors—most notably Connie's visitor—but the visitors are not interpreted in the same way I interpret them, and minimal explanation is offered. Therese E. Higgins in her chapter "*Paradise:* The Final Frontier," for example, identifies Connie's visitor as a god and perhaps the male counterpart of Connie.

5. Oddly, I have come across several articles on *Paradise* that simply identify Consolata as being from South America, when the text clearly invokes Brazil. Mary Magna and the other nuns spend twelve years in a Portuguese Order of nuns. Brazil is the only South American country colonized by Portugal. Furthermore, Consolata leads the Convent women through an initiation that closely mirrors the Afro-Brazilian religion Candomblé.

6. Susan Strehle also notes the connection between Consolata's lip biting and the desire to be homed, but she does not offer analysis of what drives Consolata's perception that Deacon can home her.

7. Francis Barker, Peter Hulme, and Margaret Iversen, eds., *Cannibalism and the Colonial World* (Cambridge, UK: Cambridge UP, 1998), 6.

8. These references are mere examples of a plethora of laws and injunctions that governed interracial relationships and marriage in the United States.

9. Sollors explains that in 1863 George Wakeman and David Goodman Croly made up the word "miscegenation" (from the Latin *miscere*, "to mix," and *genus* "race").

10. K.D.'s birth name is Coffee Morgan Smith, so his father married a Morgan just as his uncle married a Smith.

11. Chesnutt later adopts an anti-expansionist rhetoric when he recognizes that little is being done at home to uplift non-white Americans. This political shift is strongly influenced by the Spanish-American War and U.S. expansion to the Philippines.

12. I am not alone in my belief that there is no "white" girl at the Convent. Richard Schur echoes this belief in his essay "Locating *Paradise* in the Post–Civil Rights Era: Toni Morrison and Critical Race Theory."

13. This sound is also the name of an indigenous Brazilian dance. The sha, sha, sha is the sound the dancers' shoes make as they move across the ground.

14. I cite Joan Dayan's description and interpretation of Ezili, but it is important to note that she explains that her spelling of *Ezili*, *lwa*, and *Vodou* are the standard, popular Haitian spellings. Her choice in orthography is to avoid switching between French transliterations of Creole and the vast range of Gallicized Creole, which can be taxing for readers.

15. See Hazel Carby, *Reconstructing Womanhood: The Emergence of the Afro-American Woman Novelist*.

16. See "Betwixt and Between: The Liminal Period in Rites de Passage," from *The Forest of Symbols: Aspects of Ndembu Ritual* (1967), "Liminality and Communitas," from *The Ritual Process: Structure and Anti-Structure* (1969), and "Passages, Margins, and Poverty: Religious Symbols of Communitas," from *Dramas, Fields, and Metaphors* (1974).

17. The Oven debate is about the words on the lip of the oven that wore off over time, leaving the phrase indiscernible and an ugly point of contention between the adults and youth in Ruby. The adults and the teenagers develop two opposing interpretations of their meaning, which causes friction and even threats of violence.

18. I believe it is worthwhile to argue that Dovey's visitor must not only have been black, but must also have had features that resembled Ruby residents. The town's intolerance of outsiders would have surely led Dovey to feel alarmed if the visitor did not appear to be an 8-rock.

19. For specific details on the initiation rites of Candomblé see Robert Voeks, *The Sacred Leaves of Candomblé: African Magic, Medicine, and Religion in Brazil*; Rachel E. Harding, *A Refuge in Thunder: Candomblé and Alternative Spaces of Blackness*; and Shelia S. Walker, "Everyday and Esoteric Reality in the Afro-Brazilian Candomblé."

20. In *Sacred Leaves of Candomblé*, Voeks describes Yemanjá's archetype in Bahia as "the

goddess of the sea, the patron saint of fisherman. Warm, maternal, and stable, with thick bones and ample breasts . . . the archetypal symbol of fertility and motherhood" (56).

21. Fifty-two religious and philosophical texts were discovered not far from Nag Hammadi, Egypt, in 1945. The books had been buried in earthen jars for over 1,600 years. They were written in Coptic, the language spoken by Christian Egyptians.

22. The translation I consulted differs somewhat from whatever translation Morrison consulted. My translation reads:

> For many are the sweet forms that exist in numerous sins
> And unrestrained acts and disgraceful passions, and temporal pleasures,
> Which are restrained until they become sober
> And run up to their place of rest.
> And they will find me there,
> And they will live and they will not die again.

23. Here I am alluding to the title of Gloria T. Hull, Patricia Bell Scott, and Barbara Smith's pivotal black women's studies reader *All the Women Are White, All the Blacks Are Men, But Some of Us Are Brave: Black Women's Studies*.

CHAPTER TWO

1. I use both "black" and "African American" as racial descriptors because Erna Brodber was born in Jamaica, and her novel includes characters who immigrated to the United States from the Caribbean. Thus, "black" is used as a way of describing both indigenized African Americans as well as first- and second-generation Caribbean immigrants.

2. St. Clair Drake, Allison Davis, W. Montague Cobb, and Caroline Bond Day were all pre–World War II anthropologists who did antiracist work, and, though often overlooked until recently, W. E. B. Du Bois did craniometrical and public health research that refuted racial science. See Faye V. Harrison's "The Persistent Power of 'Race' in the Cultural and Political Economy of Racism" for a historical overview of how race has been approached in anthropology.

3. See Steven Gregory and Roger Sanjek's edited collection, *Race* (1994); Faye V. Harrison's *Outsider Within: Reworking Anthropology in the Global Age* (2008); and Lee D. Baker's *From Savage to Negro: Anthropology and the Construction of Race, 1896–1954* (1998) as examples of the many socio-anthropological texts addressing racism and anthropology published in the last twenty years.

4. For further reading, Bolles suggests Faye V. Harrison's "The Persistent Power of 'Race' in the Cultural and Political Economy of Racism."

5. For specific analyses of black feminist work in anthropology, see Irma McClaurin's edited collection *Black Feminist Anthropology: Theory, Politics, Praxis, and Poetics*.

6. The Black Women's Literary Renaissance began in the early 1970s with significant

literary productions by black women and much needed literary criticism on black women's writing.

7. Black women's club movements were a popular space for such racial uplift work. Many of these women paid particular attention to education, suffrage, temperance, and sometimes lynching.

8. Paule Marshall refers to the literary narratives produced by black women during the 1970s as efforts to "set the record straight," meaning that they told the stories of lives that had been ignored, or at best had received minimal attention in the white mainstream and the black male literary traditions. See Dance's interview with Marshall, 5.

9. In the essay "How It Feels to Be Colored Me," Zora Neale Hurston insists that her color does not make her tragic—she does not feel the duality of W. E. B. Du Bois's "twoness" (153).

10. *Fire!!* was a quarterly geared toward the younger "Negro" artist, and was intended to offer an alternative aesthetic to that of W. E. B. Du Bois and Alain Locke.

11. Hurston had three gripes about Thompson that she expressed to Hughes in a letter: Hughes wanted a three-way split with Louise; he proposed paying Thompson a higher than normal typist fee; he proposed Thompson be made the business manager of the Broadway production (Hemenway 141).

12. For more details on the fallout, see Hemenway's *Zora Neale Hurston: A Literary Biography* and Rachel Cohen's *A Chance Meeting: Intertwined Lives of American Artists and Writers, 1854–1967.*

13. Washington notes that Robert Stepto was the first critic to raise the question regarding Janie's voice (244).

14. While the term "West Indian" has fallen out of fashion, I use it here because that is how Brodber describes Afro-Caribbean characters in the novel.

CHAPTER THREE

1. While this project remains concerned about what space African American women occupy in transnational studies, when discussing popular culture and especially hip-hop the descriptor "African American" is limiting. The strong historical and contemporary presence of Afro-Caribbean and even Afro-British artists in the defining of hip-hop culture makes the more general racial descriptor "black" more suitable for this discussion. In using "black," however, I nonetheless maintain my focus on U.S. blacks and their invisibility in transnational studies and discourse.

2. I am thankful to Sherrod Williams for this pointed response.

3. Aside from the Beyoncé and Shakira collaboration, a similar and equally interesting collaboration is Missy "Misdemeanor" Elliot's collaboration with Nelly Furtado on the "Get Your Freak On" remix. The latter is a particularly interesting because Elliot does not have the sex-icon status of Beyoncé. Missy's music, however, consists mostly of her boasting about her abilities to deliver sex, if not sexiness, thus raising the question of whether she ought to be read as non-woman because of her pimping of sex.

4. Her choice to compose a song whose title translates as "gypsy love" is intriguing when considering Beyoncé's portrayal of Carmen, who originally was a gypsy, in *Carmen: A Hip-hopera*. This is a precursor to her collaboration with Shakira because, while there is no appropriation of Latinidad, there is a precursor of the orientalism that Shakira and Beyoncé perform in "Beautiful Liar."

5. I am thankful for Julio Javier Aguayo's translation of the lyrics from Spanish to English.

6. See Brooks, "'It's Not Right, But It's Okay': Contemporary Black Women's R&B and the House that Terry McMillan Built."

7. In addition to hooks's analysis, a number of other scholars have contributed important work attending to the ways in which black women performers, especially in hip-hop, negotiate gender politics, spectatorship, and performance: Rana Emerson's "'Where My Girls At'? Negotiating Black Womanhood in Music Videos"; Robin Roberts's "Music Videos, Performance and Resistance: Feminist Rappers"; Diane Railton's and Paul Watson's "Naughty Girls and Red Blooded Women: Representations of Female Heterosexuality in Music Video"; Murali Balaji's "Vixen Resistin': Redefining Black Womanhood in Hip-Hop Music Videos"; Patricia Hill Collins's *Black Sexual Politics: African Americans, Gender, and the New Racism*; Gwendolyn Pough's *Check It While I Wreck It: Black Womanhood, Hip-Hop, and the Public Sphere*; and T. Denean Sharpley-Whiting's *Pimps Up, Ho's Down: Hip-Hop's Hold on Young Black Women*.

8. www.mediatraffic.de/records.htm.

9. For further discussion of the accusation, see Jabari Asim's op-ed in *The Washington Post,* "Bleaching Beyoncé."

10. It is worth noting that for Shakira's Asia/Middle East tour, she lost her blonde hair, making herself more "user-friendly" for that particular audience.

11. *The Observer,* 3 January 2004, observer.guardian.co.uk/race/story/0,,1115730,00.html.

12. www.parade.com/articles/editions/2007/edition_04-15-2007/Personality_Parade.

13. Allison Samuels, "Time to Tell It Like It Is."

14. "Bills, Bills, Bills" was a hit single on the 1999 Destiny's Child sophomore album, *The Writing's on the Wall.*

15. Shakira (feat. Wyclef Jean), "Hips Don't Lie," *Oral Fixation,* Vol. 2 (Sony Music Entertainment, 2006).

16. Snoop Dogg (feat. Pharell and Uncle Charlie Wilson), "Beautiful," *Paid Da Cost to Be Da Bo$$* (Priority Records, 2002).

17. Scholars and journalists who do work on sex tourism in Brazil in particular have addressed tensions between African American and Latina/Latin American women. Jelani Cobb's *Essence* magazine article, "Blame It on Rio"; Jewel Woods and Karen Hunter's book *Don't Blame It on Rio: The Real Deal Behind Why Men Go to Brazil for Sex*; and a chapter of T. Denean Sharpley-Whiting's *Pimps Up, Ho's Down: Hip-Hop's Hold on Young Black Women* all address the twenty-first-century phenomenon of African American men flocking to Brazil, deeming it a sexual paradise where their wildest fantasies can come true at minimal financial cost.

18. Jazmine Sullivan, "Bust Your Windows," *Fearless* (J Records/Sony BMG Music Entertainment, 2008).

19. Blu Cantrell, "Hit 'Em Up Style (Oops!)," *So Blue* (Arista, 2001).

CHAPTER FOUR

1. This movement and the nationalism that it celebrated coincided with Vargas's campaign for immigrant assimilation, especially Japanese immigrants who were perceived as dangerous because of their "clannishness" and resistance to assimilation.

2. Abbott is one of many black men from the United States who visited Brazil during the 1920s and 1930s. Theodore Roosevelt's visit to Brazil in 1913 and his subsequent report, published in *Outlook* and reprinted in numerous black newspapers, struck a chord with black emigrationists like Abbott because the report affirmed that U.S. segregation and anti-miscegenation laws were not universal. The warning from a Brazilian statesman that the way the United States dealt with race was dangerous was particularly compelling for people like Abbott. See David J. Hellwig, ed. *African-American Reflections on Brazil's Racial Paradise.*

3. Skidmore notes that no bills barring black immigration were actually passed, perhaps due to black immigration not seeming to be a real threat (198–99). Meade and Pirio, however, do note that "Bahia Law N. 1729, passed on August 23, 1924 . . . stated that the immigration service sought 'to promote the settlement of Brazilians and of acceptable foreigners of the white race . . .'" (93).

4. While working for the U.S. Department of Labor, Daniel Patrick Moynihan was commissioned to write a report on the black family. The report is officially titled "The Negro Family: A Case for National Action," but is popularly referred to as the Moynihan Report.

5. Many scholars have addressed Ursa's reunification with Mutt and repetition in this text, but two classic essays are Madhu Dubey's "Gayl Jones and the Matrilineal Metaphor of Tradition" and Bruce Simon's "Traumatic Repetition: Gayl Jones's *Corregidora.*"

6. Spillers, "Mama's Baby, Papa's Maybe."

7. It also explains why, once Birdie finds her father, she sees herself in him and he sees himself, or at least his mother, in her (330, 337).

CHAPTER FIVE

1. The 1990s was the era of *New Jack City, Boyz n the Hood,* and *Juice,* just to name a few of the gangster-themed films set in urban settings.

2. Matty Rich's *The Inkwell* is another notable exception.

3. For more on African Americans on television in the post-nationalist era, see Mark Anthony Neal, *Soul Babies: Black Popular Culture and the Post-Soul Aesthetic.* A proliferation of black sitcoms became popular in the twenty-first century on the new channel UPN.

4. In his classic *The Souls of Black Folk* (1903) Du Bois prophetically declared in the Forethought the problem of the twentieth century would be the problem of the color line.

5. This shift is also reflected in the debates in *Black Film Review.*

6. In "Remembering and Repeating in *Eve's Bayou*," Kimberlyn Leary presents a conflicted interpretation when she first declares that the film "[t]ells something of a universal story" and then later proclaims that the film possesses "a unique African-American sensibility" that makes it a *black* film (195, 196). Mia Mask's review essay, "*Eve's Bayou:* Too Good to Be a 'Black' Film?" addresses the film's crossover appeal, noting that film critics "[r]einscribe the hegemony of whiteness as the locus of universal humanism" when they insist on celebrating *Eve's Bayou's* universal accessibility (26).

7. When marketing her film, Lemmons initially described her intended viewing audience as black college graduates. Because such assertions quickly ended her meetings with film executives, she switched her intended audience to that of *Waiting to Exhale.* She surmises that the "cha-ching" factor proved much more effective (Alexander, WWMM 261–62).

8. For an exception see, Michael Awkward's "Black Male Trouble: The Challenges of Rethinking Masculine Differences."

9. In this chapter, I use "black" interchangeably with "African American," because so many of the texts I cite and discourses I engage tend to use "black" instead of "African American."

10. The heading for this section is from Gayl Jones, *Song for Anninho.* To "have it all" became a third-wave feminist mantra at the turn of the twenty-first century. It became a vexed question for U.S. black women in particular, which is addressed in the interrogative title of Veronica Chamber's *Having It All? Black Women and Success* (2003), for example.

11. I use the 14 April 1994 second draft of *Eve's Bayou* script for this quote.

12. Roz has to work against the image of the asexual mammy, the hyper-sexualized Jezebel, and the mouthy Sapphire.

13. In his critical memoir, *New Black Man,* black popular culture scholar Mark Anthony Neal discusses the trouble with the idea of a "Strong Black Man."

14. Also see Awkward's *Negotiating Difference: Race, Gender, and the Politics of Positionality,* especially chapter 1.

15. Madison performs a Freudian and Lacanian reading of the film, drawing on theories of the phallus, and the mirror and jouissance.

16. Incest is a familiar trope in Faulkner's fiction. It is also familiar in African American women's writing, as witnessed in *Paradise, Corregidora,* and now *Eve's Bayou.* The narrative of a slave master fathering both his daughter and his granddaughter that appears in *Go Down, Moses* also frames *Corregidora.* This alarming trope reflects the ways in which African American women writers have been invested in ensuring that a story is told and never forgotten about the connections between the bodies of African American women, geography, and power.

17. In interviews Lemmons notes that studio people would ask her to put in a white character, even if that character was negative. Lemons declined steadfastly, insisting "This is *Eve's* bayou."

18. The Electra complex is said to be the counterpart to the Oedipus complex in males. Drawing on his theory of "penis envy," Sigmund Freud proposes that, when daughters real-

ize they do not have a penis, daughters become envious of their fathers' penis and dream of becoming pregnant by him. These feelings create hostility toward the mother who the daughter was attached to prior to her revelation. The daughter resents her mother, because she believes the mother caused her castration.

19. In "Sisters, Fathers, and the Modern Ethnic Family: *Double Happiness* and *Eve's Bayou*," Eva Reuschmann argues that both Cisely and Eve have an Oedipal competition for their father, but she does not actually discuss the Electra complex.

20. The heading of this section is from Langston Hughes, *Fine Clothes to the Jew.*

21. In "Remembering and Repeating in *Eve's Bayou*," Kimberlyn Leary briefly notes the significance of trains in the film, but her focus is on the tracks symbolizing Louis's transition from life to death.

22. Perhaps the child that is struck by the bus is one of Louis's "outside children."

23. In his critical memoir, *New Black Man,* Neal proposes that the longstanding ideal of "Strong Black Men" as race and civic leaders is in fact damaging to both black men and the larger black community.

WORKS CITED

Alexander, George. *Why We Make Movies: Black Filmmakers Talk About the Magic of Cinema*. New York: Harlem Moon, 2003.

Andrade, Mário de. Trans. E.A. Goodland. *Macunaíma*. New York: Random House, 1984.

Andrade, Oswald de. Trans. Leslie Bary. *Latin American Review*. 19.38 (1991): 38–47.

Appadurai, Arjun. *Modernity at Large: Cultural Dimensions of Globalization*. Minneapolis: U of Minnesota P, 1996.

Appiah, Kwame Anthony. *The Ethics of Identity*. Princeton, NJ: Princeton UP, 2007.

Arias, Claudia M. Milian. "An Interview with Danzy Senna." *Callaloo* 25.2 (2002): 447–52.

Arlidge, John. "Forget Black, Forget White. EA Is What's Hot." *The Observer*. London. 3 January 2004. Online.

Asim, Jabari. "Bleaching Beyoncé." *The Washington Post*, 24 October 2005. Print.

Awkward, Michael. "Black Feminism and the Challenge of Black Heterosexual Male Desire." *The New Black Renaissance: The Souls Anthology of Critical African-American Studies*, ed. Manning Marable et al. Boulder, CO: Paradigm Publishers, 2005. 137–41.

———. "Black Male Trouble: The Challenges of Rethinking Masculine Differences." *Masculinity Studies and Feminist Theory: New Directions*, ed. Judith Kegan Gardiner. New York: Columbia UP, 2002. 290–304.

———. "A Black Man's Place(s) in Black Feminist Criticism." *Who Can Speak? Authority and Critical Identity*, ed. Judith Roof and Robyn Wiegman. Urbana: U of Illinois P, 1995. 70–92.

———. *Negotiating Difference: Race, Gender, and the Politics of Positionality*. Chicago: U of Chicago P, 1995.

Baker, Lee D. *From Savage to Negro: Anthropology and the Construction of Race, 1896–1954*. Berkeley: U of California P, 1998.

Balaji, Murali. "Vixen Resistin': Redefining Black Womanhood in Hip-Hop Music Videos." *Journal of Black Studies* 41.1 (2010): 5–20.

Baldwin, James. *Go Tell It on the Mountain*. New York: Dial P, 1978.

Barker, Francis, Peter Hulme, and Margaret Iversen, eds. *Cannibalism and the Colonial World*. Cambridge, UK: Cambridge UP, 1998.

Bartolovich, Crystal. "Consumerism, or the Cultural Logic of Late Cannibalism." *Cannibalism and the Colonial World*, ed. Francis Barker, Peter Hulme, and Margaret Iversen. Cambridge, UK: Cambridge UP, 1998.

Bary, Leslie. "Oswald de Andrade's 'Cannibalist Manifesto.'" *Latin American Literary Review* 19.38 (1991): 35–37.

"Beautiful Crossover: Q and A with Beyoncé." Latina.com, latina.com/latina/entertainment/entertainment.jsp?genre=music&article=musica . . . Accessed 1 January 2008.

Bernabé, Jean, Patrick Chamoiseau, and Raphaël Confiant. "In Praise of Creoleness." *Callaloo* 13.4 (1990): 886–909.

Bhabha, Homi K. *The Location of Culture*. New York: Routledge, 1994.

Bobo, Jacqueline. "The Politics of Interpretation: Black Critics, Filmmakers, Audiences." *Black Popular Culture*, ed. Gina Dent. New York: The New Press, 1998.

———. "Sifting Through the Controversy: Reading *The Color Purple*." *Callaloo* 39 (1989): 332–42.

Bolles, A. Lynn. "Seeking the Ancestors: Forging a Black Feminist Tradition in Anthropology." *Black Feminist Anthropology: Theory, Politics, Praxis, and Poetics*, ed. Irma McClaurin. New Brunswick, NJ: Rutgers UP, 2001. 24–48.

Bouson, J. Brooks. *Quiet As It's Kept: Shame, Trauma, and Race in the Novels of Toni Morrison*. Albany: State U of New York P, 2000.

Brah, Avtar. *Cartographies of Diaspora: Contesting Identities*. London: Routledge, 1996.

Braxton, Joanne M., and Andrée Nicola McLaughlin, eds. *Wild Women in the Whirlwind: Afra-American Culture and the Contemporary Literary Renaissance*. New Brunswick, NJ: Rutgers UP, 1990.

Brodber, Erna. "Fiction in the Scientific Procedure." *Caribbean Women Writers: Essays from the First International Conference*, ed. Selwyn R. Cudjoe. Wellesley, MA: Calaloux, 1990. 164–68.

———. *Louisiana: A Novel*. Jackson: UP of Mississippi, 1994.

———. "Where Are All the Others?" *Caribbean Creolization: Reflections on the Cultural Dynamics of Language, Literature, and Identity*, ed. Kathleen M. Balutansky and Marie-Agnés Sourieau. Gainesville: UP of Florida, 1998.

Brooks, Daphne A. "'It's Not Right But It's Okay': Black Women's R&B and the House that Terry McMillan Built." *Souls* 5.1 (2003) 32–45.

———. "Suga Mama, Politicized." *The Nation*. 30 November 2006. www.the
nation.com/doc/20061218/brooks accessed 8 June 2007.

Cantrell, Blu. "Hit 'Em Up Style (Oops!)." *So Blue*. CD. Arista, 2001.

Carby, Hazel. *Reconstructing Womanhood: The Emergence of the Afro-American
Woman Novelist*. New York: Oxford UP, 1987.

Cepeda, Maria Elena. "Shakira as the Idealized, Transnational Citizen: A Case
Study of *Colombianidad* in Transition. *Latino Studies* 1 (2003): 211–32.

Chambers, Veronica. *Having It All? Black Women and Success*. New York: Doubleday, 2003.

Chesnutt, Charles W. "The Future American: What the Race Is Likely to Become
in the Process of Time." *Charles W. Chesnutt: Essays and Speeches*, ed. Joseph R.
McElrath Jr., Robert C. Leitz III, and Jesse S. Crisler. Palo Alto, CA: Stanford
UP, 1999. 131–35.

Chopin, Kate. "Desiree's Baby." Ed. Judith Baxter. *The Awakening: and Other Stories*. Cambridge, U.K.: Cambridge UP, 1996.

Chow, Rey. "When Whiteness Feminizes . . . : Some Consequences of a Supple-
mentary Logic." *Differences* 11.3 (1999): 137–68.

Cobb, Jelani. "Blame it on Rio." *Essence* 37.5 (Sept. 2006): 204, 206–8, 258.

Cohen, Cathy J. "Punks, Bulldaggers, and Welfare Queens: The Radical Potential
of Queer Politics." *GLQ: A Journal of Lesbian and Gay Studies* 3.4 (May 1997):
437–65.

Cohen, Rachel. *A Chance Meeting: Intertwined Lives of American Writers and Artists,
1854–1967*. New York: Random House, 2004.

Collins, Patricia Hill. *Black Feminist Thought: Knowledge, Consciousness, and the
Politics of Empowerment*. New York: Routledge, 1991.

———. *Black Sexual Politics: African Americans, Gender, and the New Racism*. New
York: Routledge, 2004.

———. *From Black Power to Hip Hop: Racism, Nationalism, and Feminism*. Philadelphia: Temple UP, 2006.

Dance, Daryl Cumber. "An Interview with Paule Marshall." *Southern Review* 28
(1992): 1–20.

Davies, Carole Boyce. *Black Women, Writing, and Identity: Migrations of the Subject*.
London: Routledge, 1994.

Dayan, Joan. *Haiti, History, and the Gods*. Berkeley: U of California P, 1995.

Deren, Maya. *Divine Horsemen: The Living Gods of Haiti*. 1953. New York: McPher-
son & Co., 1970.

Destiny's Child. "Bills, Bills, Bills." *The Writing's on the Wall*. CD. Sony BMG Music
Entertainment, 1999.

Du Bois, W. E. B. *The Souls of Black Folk*. New York: Vintage Books, 1990.

Dubey, Madhu. "Gayl Jones and the Matrilineal Metaphor of Tradition." *Signs* 20.2 (Winter 1995): 245–67.

———. "Postmodernism as Postnationalism? Racial Representation in U.S. Black Cultural Studies." *The Black Scholar* 33.1 (2003): 2–18.

duCille, Ann. *Skin Trade*. Cambridge, MA: Harvard UP, 1996.

Dussere, Erik. *Balancing the Books: Faulkner, Morrison, and the Economies of Slavery*. New York: Routledge, 2003.

Edwards, Brent Hayes. *The Practice of Diaspora: Literature, Translation, and the Rise of Black Internationalism*. Cambridge, MA: Harvard UP, 2003.

Emerson, Rana A. "'Where My Girls At?': Negotiating Black Womanhood in Music Videos." *Gender & Society* 16.1 (2002): 115–35.

Eve's Bayou. Dir. Kasi Lemmons. Film. Trimark Pictures. 1997.

Faulkner, William. *Go Down, Moses*. 1940. New York: Vintage Books, 1970.

Fishkin, Shelley Fisher. "Crossroads of Cultures: The Transnational Turn in American Studies—Presidential Address to the American Studies Association, November 12, 2004." *American Quarterly* 57.1 (2005): 17–57.

Freyre, Giberto. *The Master and Slaves (Casa Grande & Senzala): A Study in the Development of Brazilian Civilization*. Berkeley: U of California P, 1986.

Gates, Henry Louis, Jr. *Figures in Black: Words, Signs, and the "Racial" Self*. New York: Oxford UP, 1987.

———. *The Signifying Monkey: A Theory of Afro-American Literary Criticism*. New York: Oxford UP, 1988.

Gilroy, Paul. *Against Race: Imagining Political Culture Beyond the Color Line*. Cambridge, MA: Harvard UP, 2000.

———. "Route Work: The Black Atlantic and Politics of Exile." *The Post-Colonial Question: Common Skies, Divided Horizons*, ed. Iain Chambers and Lidia Curti. London: Routledge, 1996.

Gordon, Avery F. *Ghostly Matters: Haunting and the Sociological Imagination*. Minneapolis: U of Minnesota P, 1997.

Gottfried, Amy S. "Angry Arts: Silence, Speech, and Song in Gayl Jones's *Corregidora*." *African American Review* 28.4 (1994): 559–70.

Gregory, Steven, and Roger Sanjek, eds. *Race*. New Brunswick, NJ: Rutgers UP, 1994.

Griffin, Farah Jasmine. "That the Mothers May Soar and the Daughters May Know Their Names: A Retrospective of Black Feminist Literary Criticism." *Signs* 32.2 (2007): 483–507.

Gubar, Susan. "What Ails Feminist Criticism?" *Critical Inquiry* 24.4 (1998): 878–902.

Gupta, Akhil, and James Ferguson, eds. "Discipline and Practice: The Field as Site, Method, and Location in Anthropology." *Anthropological Locations: Boundaries and Grounds of a Field Science.* Berkeley: U of California P, 1997. 1–46.

———. "Whither Black Women's Studies: Interview." *Differences* 9.3 (1997): 31–45.

Guzmán, Isabel Molina, and Angharad N. Valdivia. "Brain, Brow, and Booty: Latina Iconicity in U.S. Popular Culture." *The Communication Review* 7.2 (2004): 205–21.

Hall, Stuart. "Cultural Identity and Diaspora." *Colonial Discourse and Post-colonial Theory: A Reader,* ed. Patrick Williams and Laura Chrisman. New York: Columbia UP, 1994. 392–403.

Hammonds, E. M., Guy-Sheftall, Beverly. "Response from a "Second Waver" to Kimberly Springer's "Third Wave Black Feminism?" *Signs* 27.4 (2002): 1091–94.

Hanchard, Michael, ed. *Racial Politics in Contemporary Brazil.* Durham, NC: Duke UP, 1999.

Harding, Rachel E. *A Refuge in Thunder: Candomblé and Alternative Spaces of Blackness.* Bloomington: Indiana UP, 2000.

Hardy, Ernest. "I, Too, Sing Hollywood: Four Women on Race, Art and Making Movies." *LA Weekly.* 18 October 2000. www.laweekly.com/general/features/i-too-sing-hollywood/5356/.

Harris, Trudier, "This Disease Called Strength: Some Observations on the Compensating Construction of Black Female Character." *Literature and Medicine* 14.1 (1995): 109–126.

Harrison, Faye V. *Outsider Within: Reworking Anthropology in the Global Age.* Urbana: U Illinois P, 2008.

———. "The Persistent Power of 'Race' in the Cultural and Political Economy of Racism." *Annual Review of Anthropology* 24 (1995): 47–74.

Harrison-Kahan, Lori. "Passing for White, Passing for Jewish: Mixed Race Identity in Danzy Senna and Rebecca Walker." *MELUS* 30.1 (2005): 19–48.

Hartman, Saidiya. *Lose Your Mother: A Journey Along the Atlantic Slave Route.* New York: Farrar, Straus and Giroux, 2007.

Hawkins, Stephanie L. "Building the 'Blue' Race: Miscegenation, Mysticism, and the Language of Cognitive Evolution in Jean Toomer's 'The Blue Meridian.'" *Texas Studies in Literature and Language* 46.2 (2004): 149–80. Project Muse. 23 November 2005. muse.jhu.edu.

Hellwig, David J., ed. *African-American Reflections on Brazil's Racial Paradise.* Philadelphia: Temple UP, 1992.

Hemenway, Robert E. *Zora Neale Hurston: A Literary Biography.* Urbana: U of Illinois P, 1977.

Henry, Astrid. *Not My Mother's Sister: Generational Conflict and Third-Wave Feminism*. Bloomington: Indiana UP, 2004.

Hernández, Daisy, and Bushra Rehman. *Colonize This!: Young Women of Color on Today's Feminism*. New York: Seal P, 2002.

Higgins, Therese E. *Religiosity, Cosmology, and Folklore: The African Influence in the Novels of Toni Morrison*. New York: Routledge, 2001.

Hine, Darlene Clark, et al., ed. *African-American Odyssey*. 2nd ed. Upper Saddle River, NJ: Prentice Hall, 2003.

———. *Hine Sight: Black Women and the Re-Construction of American History*. Bloomington: Indiana UP, 1997.

Holland, Sharon. "On Waiting to Exhale: Or What To Do When You're Feeling Black and Blue, A Review of Recent Black Feminist Criticism." *Feminist Studies* 26.1 (2000): 101–12.

———. *Raising the Dead: Readings of Death and (Black) Subjectivity*. Durham, NC: Duke UP, 2000.

Holloway, Karla F. C. "'Cruel Enough to Stop the Blood': Global Feminisms and the U.S. Body Politic, Or: 'They Done Taken My Blues and Gone.'" *Meridians: Feminism, Race, Transnationalism* 7.1 (2006): 1–18.

hooks, bell. *All About Love: New Visions*. New York: Perennial, 2001.

———. *Black Looks: Race and Representation*. Boston: South End P, 1992.

Hughes, Langston. *Fine Clothes to the Jew*. New York: A. A. Knopf, 1927.

Hull, Gloria T., et al., ed. *All the Women Are White, All the Blacks Are Men, But Some of Us Are Brave: Black Women's Studies*. New York: Feminist P at CUNY, 1982.

Hurston, Zora Neale. "How It Feels to Be Colored Me." *I Love Myself When I Am Laughing . . . And Then Again When I Am Looking Mean and Impressive*. Ed. Alice Walker. New York: Feminist P, 1979. 152–55.

———. *Tell My Horse: Voodoo and Life in Haiti and Jamaica*. 1938. New York: Perennial Library, 1990.

———. *Their Eyes Were Watching God*. 1937. New York: Harper & Row, 1990.

Jones, Carolyn M. "Imagining Race and Religion in Louisiana: Kasi Lemmons's *Eve's Bayou* and Barbara Hambly's Benjamin January Novels." *Religion in the Contemporary South: Changes, Continuities, and Contexts*, ed. Corrie E. Norman and Don S. Armentrout. Knoxville: U of Tennessee P, 2005.

Jones, Gayl. *Corregidora*. Boston: Beacon P, 1975.

———. *Song for Anninho*. Detroit: Lotus P, 1981.

Kawash, Samira. *Dislocating the Color Line: Identity, Hybridity, and Singularity in African-American Narrative*. Stanford, CA: Stanford UP, 1997.

Keft-Kennedy, Virginia. "'How Does She Do That?' Belly Dancing and the Horror of a Flexible Woman." *Women's Studies* 34.3–4 (2005): 279–300.

Kinser, Amber E. "Negotiating Space for/through Third-Wave Feminism." *NWSA Journal* 16.3 (2004): 124–53.

Knowles, Beyoncé, and Shakira. "Beautiful Liar." CD single, digital download. Sony Music Studios, 2007.

Kobayashi, Audrey, and Linda Peake. "Racism Out of Place: Thoughts on Whiteness and an Antiracist Geography in the New Millennium." *Annals of the Association of American Geographers* 90.2 (2002): 392–403.

La Ferla, Ruth. "Generation E.A. Ethnically Ambiguous." *New York Times*. 28 December 2003. www.nytimes.com/2003/72/28/style/generation-era-ethnically -ambiguous.html.

Larsen, Nella. *Quicksand and Passing.* Ed. Deborah McDowell. 1986. New Brunswick, NJ: Rutgers UP, 2004.

Leary, Kimberlyn. "Remembering and Repeating in Eve's Bayou." *Psychoanalysis and Film*, ed. Glen O. Gabbard. New York: Karnac Books, 2001. 193–200.

LeClair, Thomas. "The Language Must Not Sweat: A Conversation with Toni Morrison." *New Republic* 184 (21 March 1981): 25–29.

Lemmons, Kasi. *Eve's Bayou.* Screenplay. 2nd draft, 1994.

Levander, Caroline F., and Robert S. Levine. "Introduction: Hemispheric American Literary History." *American Literary History* 18.3 (2006): 397–405. PDF.

Lorde, Audre. *Sister Outsider: Essays and Speeches, 1984. Freedom, CA: Crossing Press, 1996.*

Luis-Brown, David. *Waves of Decolonization: Discourses of Race and Hemispheric Citizenship in Cuba, Mexico, and the United States.* Durham, NC: Duke UP, 2008.

Madison, D. Soyini. "Oedipus Rex At *Eve's Bayou* Or The Little Black Girl Who Left Sigmund Freud in the Swamp." *Cultural Studies* 14.2 (2000): 311–40.

Marks, Donald R. "Sex, Violence, and Organic Consciousness in Zora Neale Hurston's *Their Eyes Were Watching God.*" *Black American Literature Forum* 19.4 (Winter 1985): 152–57.

Marshall, Paule. *Praisesong for the Widow.* New York: Penguin, 1983.

Mask, Mia. "Eve's Bayou: Too Good To Be a 'Black' Film?" *Cineaste* 23.4 (1998): 26–28.

McClaurin, Irma, ed. *Black Feminist Anthropology: Theory, Politics, Praxis, and Poetics.* New Brunswick, NJ: Rutgers UP, 2001.

McDowell, Deborah E. "New Directions for Black Feminist Criticism." *Black American Literature Forum* 14.4 (Winter 1980): 153–59.

McHenry, Elizabeth. *Forgotten Readers: Recovering the Lost History of African American Literary Societies.* Durham, N.C.: Duke UP, 2002.

Meade, Teresa, and Gregory Alonso Pirio. "In Search of the Afro-American 'Eldorado': Attempts by North American Blacks to Enter Brazil in the 1920s." *Luso-Brazilian Review* 25.1 (1988): 85–110.

Millichamp, Joseph R. *Dixie Limited: Railroads, Culture, and the Southern Renaissance.* Lexington: UP of Kentucky, 2002.

Morgan, Joan. *When Chickenheads Come Home to Roost: My Life As A Hip-Hop Feminist.* New York: Simon & Schuster, 1999.

Morrison, Toni. *Beloved.* New York, Plume, 1988.

———. "Home." *The House that Race Built: Black Americans, U.S. Terrain,* ed. Wahneema Lubiano. New York: Pantheon Books, 1997. 3–12.

———. "Nobel Lecture." Nobelprize.org. 16 Apr 2013. www.nobelprize.org/nobel _prizes/literature/laureates/1993/morrison-lecture.html.

———. *Paradise.* New York: Knopf, 1997.

———. *Tar Baby.* New York: Knopf, 1981.

———. "Unspeakable Things Unspoken: The Afro-American Presence in American Literature." *Michigan Quarterly Review* 28.1 (1989): 1–34.

Moynihan, Daniel Patrick. *The Negro Family: The Case for National Action.* U.S. Department of Labor. 1965. www.dol.gov/oasam/programs/history/webid -meynihan.htm.

Mullings, Leith. "Interrogating Racism: Toward an Antiracist Anthropology." *Annual Review of Anthropology* 34 (2005): 667–93.

Nag Hammadi. "Thunder: Perfect Mind." gnosis.org/naghamm/thunder.html. Cited in *The Nag Hammadi Library,* ed. James M. Robinson. Rev. ed. San Francisco: HarperCollins, 1990.

Narain, Denise deCaires. "The Body of the Woman in the Body of the Text: The Novels of Erna Brodber." *Caribbean Women Writers: Fiction in English,* ed. Mary Conde and Thorunn Lonsdale. New York: St. Martin's P, 1999. 97–116.

Neal, Mark Anthony. "Getting Grown." *PopMatters.* www.popmatters.com/music /reviews/b/Beyoncé-dangerously.shtml. Retrieved 10 September 2010.

———. *New Black Man.* New York: Routledge, 2005.

———. *Soul Babies: Black Popular Culture and the Post-Soul Aesthetic.* New York: Routledge, 2002.

N.O.R.E. feat. Nina Sky and Daddy Yankee. "Oye Mi Canto." *N.O.R.E. y la Familia . . . Ya Tú Sabe.* CD single, digital download. Island Def Jam Music Group, 2006.

Nwankwo, Ifeoma Kiddoe. *Black Cosmopolitanism: Racial Consciousness and Transnational Identity in the Nineteenth-Century Americas.* Philadelphia: U of Pennsylvania P, 2005.

Parade magazine. 15 April 2007. www.parade.com/articles/editions/2007/edition _04–15–2007/Personality_Parade.

PMLA. 121.5 (October 2006).

Pough, Gwendolyn D. *Check It While I Wreck It: Black Womanhood, Hip-Hop Culture, and the Public Sphere.* Boston: Northeastern UP, 2004.

Railton, Diane, and Paul Watson. "Naughty Girls and Red Blooded Women: Representations of Female Heterosexuality in Music Video." *Feminist Media Studies* 5.1 (2005): 51–63.

Reid-Pharr, Robert. *Conjugal Union: The Body, the House, and the Black American.* New York: Oxford UP, 1999.

Rivera, Raquel Z. *New York Ricans from the Hip Hop Zone.* New York: Palgrave Macmillan, 2003.

Rivkin, Julie, and Michael Ryan, ed. *Literary Theory: An Anthology.* Malden, MA: Blackwell Publishers, 1998.

Roberts, Robin. "Music Videos, Performance and Resistance: Feminist Rappers." *The Journal of Popular Culture.* 25.2 (Fall 1991): 141-152.

Rooks, Noliwe M. "Like Canaries in the Mines: Black Women's Studies at the Millennium." *Signs* 25.4 (2000): 1209–11.

Rosenthal, Debra J. *Race Mixture in Nineteenth-Century U.S. and Spanish American Fictions: Gender, Culture, and Nation Building.* Chapel Hill: U of North Carolina P, 2004.

Rueschmann, Eva. *Sisters on Screen: Siblings in Contemporary Cinema.* Philadelphia: Temple UP, 2000.

Samuels, Allison. "Time to Tell It Like It Is." *Newsweek,* 2 March 2003. LexisNexis Academic, online.

Sandoval, Chela. *Methodology of the Oppressed.* Minneapolis: U of Minnesota P, 2000.

Schur, Richard L. "Locating *Paradise* in the Post–Civil Rights Era: Toni Morrison and Critical Race Theory." *Contemporary Literature* 45.2 (2004): 276–99.

Schuyler, George. *Black No More.* Boston: Northeastern UP, 1989.

Senna, Danzy. *Caucasia.* New York: Riverhead Books, 1998.

———. "The Mulatto Millennium." *Half and Half: Writers on Growing Up Biracial and Bicultural,* ed. Claudine Chiawei O'Hearn. New York: Pantheon Books, 1998. 12–27.

702. "Where My Girls At?" *702.* CD. Universal Motown, 1999.

Shakira (feat. Wyclef Jean). "Hips Don't Lie." *Oral Fixation.* Vol. 2. CD, Digital download. Sony Music Entertainment, 2006.

Sharpley-Whiting, T. Denean. *Pimps Up, Ho's Down: Hip Hop's Hold on Young Black Women.* New York: New York UP, 2007.

Shay, Anthony, and Barbara Sellers-Young. "Belly Dance: Orientalism—Exoticism—Self-Exoticism." *Dance Research Journal* 35.1 (2003): 13–37.

Shepperson, George. "African Diaspora: Concept and Context." *Global Dimensions of the African Diaspora,* ed. Joseph E. Harris. Washington, DC: Howard UP, 1993. 41–50.

Simon, Bruce. "Traumatic Repetition: Gayl Jones's *Corregidora*." *Race Consciousness: African-American Studies for the New Century*, ed. Judith Jackson Fossett and Jeffrey A. Tucker. New York: New York UP, 1997. 93–112.

Skidmore, Thomas E. *Black into White: Race and Nationality in Brazilian Thought.* New York: Oxford UP, 1974.

Smith, Barbara. *The Truth That Never Hurts: Writings on Race, Gender, and Freedom.* New Brunswick, NJ: Rutgers UP, 1998.

Smith, Valerie. *Representing Blackness: Issues in Film and Video.* New Brunswick, NJ: Rutgers UP, 1997.

Snoop Dogg (feat. Pharell and Uncle Charlie Wilson). "Beautiful." *Paid Da Cost to Be Da Bo$$.* CD, digital download. Priority Records, 2002.

Sollors, Werner. *Neither Black Nor White Yet Both: Thematic Exploration of Interracial Literature.* Cambridge, MA: Harvard UP, 1997.

Soto, Sandra K. "Where in the Transnational World Are U.S. Women of Color." *Women Studies for the Future: Foundations, Interrogations, Politics*, ed. Elizabeth Lapovsky Kennedy and Agatha Beins. New Brunswick, NJ: Rutgers UP, 2005. 111–24.

Spillers, Hortense J. "Mama's Baby, Papa's Maybe: An American Grammar Book." *Diacritics* 17.2 (Summer 1987): 65–81.

Springer, Kimberly. "Third Wave Black Feminism." *Signs* 27.4 (2002): 1059–82.

Strehle, Susan. *Transnational Women's Fiction: Unsettling Home and Homeland.* New York: Palgrave Macmillan, 2008.

Sugg, Katherine. "Literatures of the Americas, *Latinidad*, and the Re-formation of Multi-Ethnic Literatures." *MELUS* 29.3–4 (2004): 227–42.

Sullivan, Jazmine, Remi Salaam, and Deandre Way. "Bust Your Windows." *Fearless.* CD, digital download. J Records/Sony BMG Music Entertainment, 2008.

Tate, Claudia, ed. *Black Women Writers at Work.* New York: Continuum, 1983.

——. *Psychoanalysis and Black Novels: Desire and the Protocols of Race.* New York: Oxford UP, 1998.

Telles, Edward Eric. *Race in Another America: The Significance of Skin Color in Brazil.* Princeton, NJ: Princeton UP, 2004.

Toomer, Jean. "The Blue Meridian." *The New Caravan*, ed. Alfred Kreymborg, Lewis Mumford, Paul Rosenfeld. New York: W. W. Norton & Co., 1936. 633–53.

Turner, Victor. *Dramas, Fields, and Metaphors: Symbolic Action in Human Society.* Ithaca: Cornell UP, 1975.

——. *The Forest of Symbols: Aspects of Ndembu Ritual.* Ithaca, NY: Cornell UP, 1970.

———. *The Ritual Process: Structure and Anti-Structure*. Piscataway, NJ: Aldine Transaction, 1995.

Voeks, Robert A. *The Sacred Leaves of Candomblé: African Magic, Medicine, and Religion in Brazil*. Austin: U of Texas P, 1997.

Walker, Alice, ed. *I Love Myself When I Am Laughing . . . and Then Again When I Am Looking Mean and Impressive*. New York: Feminist P at CUNY, 1979.

Walker, Rebecca, ed. *To Be Real: Telling the Truth and Changing the Face of Feminism*. New York: Anchor Books, 1995.

Walker, Sheila S. "Everyday and Esoteric Reality in the Afro-Brazilian Candomblé." *History of Religions* 30.2 (Nov. 1990): 103–28.

Walters, Wendy W. *At Home in Diaspora: Black International Writing*. Minneapolis: U of Minnesota P, 2005.

Wardi, Anissa Janine. "A Laying on of Hands: Toni Morrison and the Materiality of *Love*." *MELUS: The Journal of the Society for the Study of the Multi-Ethnic Literature of the United States* 30.3 (2005): 201–18.

Washington, Mary Helen, ed. *Black-Eyed Susans: Classic Stories By and About Black Women*. Garden City, NY: Anchor Books, 1975.

———. "'The Darkened Eye Restored': Notes Toward a Literary History of Black Women." *Within the Circle: An Anthology of African American Literary Criticism from the Harlem Renaissance to the Present*, ed. Angelyn Mitchell. Durham, NC: Duke UP, 1994. 442–53.

———. "'Disturbing the Peace: What Happens to American Studies If You Put African American Studies at the Center?' Presidential Address to the American Studies Association, 29 October 1997." *American Quarterly* 50.1 (1998): 1–23.

———. "I Love the Way Janie Crawford Left Her Husbands": Zora Neale Hurston's Emergent Female Hero." *Invented Lives*. New York: Doubleday, 1987. 237–54.

———. Intro. *I Love Myself When I Am Laughing . . . And Then Again When I Am Looking Mean and Impressive*, ed. Alice Walker. Old Westbury, NY: Feminist P, 1979.

———. Intro. *Their Eyes Were Watching God*. New York: Harper & Row, 1990.

———, ed. *Invented Lives: Narratives of Black Women, 1860–1960*. New York: Doubleday, 1987.

West, Cornel. *Race Matters*. Boston: Beacon P, 1993.

Wiegman, Robyn. "What Ails Feminist Criticism: A Second Opinion." *Critical Inquiry* 25.2 (1999): 362–79.

Williams, Sherley Anne. Foreword. *Their Eyes Were Watching God*. Urbana-Champaign: U of Illinois P, 1978.

Wilson, William Julius. *The Declining Significance of Race: Blacks and Changing American Institutions*. 1978. Chicago: U of Chicago P, 1980.

Woods, Jewel, and Karen Hunter. *Don't Blame It on Rio: The Real Deal Behind Why Men Go to Brazil for Sex*. New York: Grand Central Publishing, 2008.

Wright, Michelle M. *Becoming Black: Creating Identity in the African Diaspora*. Durham, NC: Duke UP, 2004.

INDEX